DRAMA CLASSICS

The Drama Classics series aims to offer the world's greatest plays in affordable paperback editions for students, actors and theatregoers. The hallmarks of the series are accessible introductions, uncluttered and uncut texts and an overall theatrical perspective.

Given that readers may be encountering a particular play for the first time, the introduction seeks to fill in the theatrical/historical background and to outline the chief themes rather than concentrate on interpretational and textual analysis. Similarly the play-texts themselves are free of footnotes and other interpolations: instead there is an end-glossary of 'difficult' words and phrases.

The texts of the English-language plays in the series have been prepared taking full account of all existing scholarship. The foreign language plays have been translated into a modern English that is both actable and accurate: most of the translations have been professionally staged.

Under the editorship of Kenneth McLeish, the Drama Classics series is building into a first-class library of dramatic literature representing the best of world theatre.

Series editor: Kenneth McLeish

Associate editors:
Professor Trevor R. Griffiths, *School of Literary and Media Studies, University of North London*

Simon Trussler, *Reader in Drama, Goldsmiths' College, University of London*

DRAMA CLASSICS *the first hundred*

The Alchemist
All for Love
Amphitryon
Andromache
Antigone
Arden of Faversham
Bacchae
The Beaux Stratagem
The Beggar's Opera
Birds
Blood Wedding
Brand
The Broken Jug
The Changeling
The Cherry Orchard
Children of the Sun
El Cid
The Country Wife
Cyrano de Bergerac
The Dance of Death
The Devil is an Ass
Doctor Faustus
A Doll's House
The Duchess of Malfi
Edward II
Electra (Euripides)
Electra (Sophocles)
An Enemy of the People
Enrico IV
The Eunuch
Every Man in his
    Humour
Everyman
The Father
Faust
A Flea in her Ear
Frogs
Fuenteovejuna
The Game of Love
    and Chance

Ghosts
The Government
    Inspector
Hedda Gabler
The Hypochondriac
The Importance of
    Being Earnest
An Italian Straw Hat
The Jew of Malta
King Oedipus
The Learned Ladies
Life is a Dream
The Lower Depths
The Lucky Chance
Lulu
Lysistrata
The Magistrate
The Malcontent
The Man of Mode
The Marriage of
    Figaro
Mary Stuart
The Master Builder
Medea
Menaechmi
The Misanthrope
The Miser
Miss Julie
Molière
A Month in the
    Country
A New Way to Pay
    Old Debts
Oedipus at Kolonos
The Oresteia
Phaedra
Philoctetes
The Playboy of the
    Western World

The Revenger's
    Tragedy
The Rivals
The Robbers
La Ronde
The Rover
The School for
    Scandal
The Seagull
The Servant of Two
    Masters
She Stoops to Conquer
The Shoemaker's
    Holiday
Six Characters in
    Search of an
    Author
Spring's Awakening
Strife
Tartuffe
Thérèse Raquin
Three Sisters
'Tis Pity She's a
    Whore
Too Clever by Half
Ubu
Uncle Vanya
Vassa Zheleznova
Volpone
The Way of the World
The White Devil
The Wild Duck
Women Beware
    Women
Women of Troy
Woyzeck
Yerma

The publishers welcome
suggestions for further titles

DRAMA CLASSICS

THE
LEARNED LADIES

by

Molière

translated by A.R. Waller
adapted by Steven Pimlott and Colin Chambers
with an introduction by Kenneth McLeish

NICK HERN BOOKS

London

in association with the

ROYAL SHAKESPEARE COMPANY

Stratford

A Drama Classic

The Learned Ladies first published in Great Britain in
this adaptation as a paperback original in 1996 by
Nick Hern Books Limited, 14 Larden Road, London W3 7ST

A.R Waller's original translation from the French of
Les Femmes Savants first published in 1907

Copyright in this adaptation © 1996 by Steven Pimlott
and Colin Chambers

Copyright in the introduction © 1996 Nick Hern Books Ltd

Typeset by Country Setting, Woodchurch, Kent TN26 3TB

Printed in Great Britain by Athenaeum Press Ltd, Gateshead,
Tyne and Wear

A CIP catalogue record for this book is available from
the British Library

ISBN 1 85459 375 7

Introduction

Molière (1622-1673)

Jean-Baptiste Poquelin (later known as Molière) was baptised on 15 January 1622; his birth-date is not known. His parents belonged to the upper-middle class; his father had made a fortune in the upholstery business and then become a courtier of King Louis XIV, being granted royal favour and the honorary position of *Tapissier du Roi* ('upholsterer royal'). Young Poquelin was given an expensive education and studied law at the university of Orléans. But from childhood, encouraged by his grandfather, he was devoted to the theatre and in 1643 he announced that he was foregoing his father's business and court position (which had been been made hereditary); instead, he asked for his inheritance in cash, put it into a newly-formed theatre company, the Illustre Théâtre, became an actor and took the stage-name Molière.

In the new company, Molière showed exceptional ability both as writer and performer. The Illustre Théâtre specialised in *commedia dell' arte*, the semi-improvised farce style imported from Italy and starring such characters as Arlecchino (Harlequin) and Colombina; Molière played Sganarelle, the leading clown. He devised scripts for these lightweight, slapstick shows, adapting Italian originals and inventing new plots and business. Only two survive: *Sooty-face is Jealous* (*La Jalousie du Barbouillé*) and *The Doctor Who Could Fly* (*Le Médicin volant*). At first the company worked in Paris, but after a few months it ran out of money, and Molière was imprisoned for debt. When he came out of prison he took the Illustre Théâtre on tour round the provinces, not returning to Paris until 1658.

Back in Paris, Molière and his company found royal patronage, from the King's brother Philippe d'Orléans. Molière's first full-length Parisian play, *The Scatterbrain* (*L'Étourdi*) was put on in 1655; in 1659 he had a success with *The Pretentious Ladies* (*Les Précieuses ridicules*), whose plot and characters anticipate those of *The Learned Ladies*, and in 1662 he repeated it with *The School for Wives* (*L'École des femmes*). In 1664 the King granted him an annual salary and did him the signal honour of acting as godfather to his first child, Louis. In 1665 Molière's company was appointed the Troupe du Roi and, despite constant intrigues and arguments with rivals, retained royal favour thereafter.

In his court plays, Molière moved away from his former *commedia dell'arte* style, except for occasional slapstick scenes. Instead, he developed a new kind of comedy in which the characters' obsessions and absurdities were not two-dimensional but psychologically complex and persuasive, and which allowed him to satirise ideas and manners of the time. In the touring plays, 'satire' might consist of such things as sending up stammerers or shy lovers; in the court plays he mocks more serious topics such as manners and etiquette, religious hypocrisy (this caused most of the scandal, as he was accused of mocking true religion), the desire for social advancement, and above all fads and fashions in the arts. This is the period of his greatest and best-known plays, *Tartuffe, Don Juan, The Misanthrope, The Miser* (*L'Avare*) – and *The Would-be Gentleman* (*Le Bourgeois gentilhomme*) and *The Hypochondriac* (*Le Malade imaginaire*), two examples of a new kind of entertainment devised with the composer Lully, 'comedy ballets' in which spoken comedy was framed by scenes of song and dance.

In 1666, in his mid-forties, Molière fell ill with pneumonia and had to give up acting for several months. (He spent the time writing.) Although when he recovered he returned to performing, his health remained precarious, and in 1673, at the fourth performance of *The Hypochondriac*, he began coughing blood in the middle of the show and reached the end only with difficulty. He was carried back to his house in the Rue de Richelieu and died soon afterwards. At first he was refused Christian burial – a fate common to actors, who at the time were regarded as living outside the blessing of the Church. Even when the King intervened, this decision was only reluctantly revoked, and Molière was given a hasty and unceremonious burial in St Joseph's cemetery in the middle of the night.

The Learned Ladies: **What Happens in the Play**

In the household of Chrysale, a rich Parisian, war rages between the worlds of the intellect and the emotions. Chrysale himself, his brother Ariste and his young friend Clitandre are ordinary people, ruled by their emotions; Chrysale's wife Philaminte, her sister-in-law Bélise and her elder daughter Armande are intellectual snobs who proclaim that nothing is important but book-learning, and that 'matters of the senses', including love, are beneath contempt. Caught in the middle is Chrysale's younger daughter Henriette. Her mother wants her to marry the pretentious poet Trissotin; she prefers Clitandre, and her father supports her choice.

As the play proceeds we learn more about the three 'learned ladies'. Bélise has long ago made the decision to spurn lovers and embrace literature – and though she feels a distinct sense of loss, she sticks to her decision. Armande, formerly betrothed to Clitandre, is happy to have rejected him until she finds out that he, in turn, has rejected her and wants to marry Henriette. As for Philaminte, she is obsessed with the idea of setting up an ideal society of philosophers, 'better even than Plato's *Republic*', and until this can come into being she contents herself with ruling her own household with a will of iron. She sacks the kitchen-maid Martine for bad grammar, decides each day which words are 'in' or 'out', and fawns on anyone with a smattering of Latin or, better still, Greek. Trissotin works his way into this ménage by gross flattery, and by insulting and routing all possible rivals (for example the Greek-speaking scholar Vadius). Philaminte will hear no criticism of him, in particular the idea that all he wants to do is marry Henriette and lay hands on her fortune. Only at the very end of the play, when Ariste tricks Trissotin into thinking that Chrysale has been bankrupted overnight, is the fraud discovered. Trissotin leaves in high dudgeon, Henriette and Clitandre are united, and everyone is able to live happily ever afterwards – or as happily as Philaminte, who has lost this battle but not the war, will let them.

The Learned Ladies

The Learned Ladies was the last-but-one of Molière's plays (followed only by *The Hypochondriac*) and the last of his great rhyming-couplet comedies. Its predecessors had used the artificiality of the style to add point and irony to some of Molière's most trenchant examinations of aspects of the human condition, for example obsessive possessiveness (in *The School for Wives*), religious hypocrisy (in *Tartuffe*) and disenchantment with life (in *The Misanthrope*). For lighter-hearted satire, sending up specific behaviour rather than the general human condition, Molière tended to use prose: examples are *George Dandin* and such 'comedy-ballets' as *The Would-be Gentleman*. *The Learned Ladies* has the best of both worlds: it satirises a specific fad (intellectual pretension) but – perhaps because its subject requires an appropriately 'high style' – is written in rhyming verse.

Molière had already hit the target of cultural snobbery thirteen years before, in his first great court success, *The Pretentious Ladies*. Like that play, *The Learned Ladies* mocks the fashion, current among upper-class ladies, for holding *salons* to discuss such 'learned' matters as the arts, philosophy and science. The joke, to Molière's audience, was not merely intellectual snobbery, but that the snobs were women. This was an age when matters of the mind were, in theory, still the province of men; upper-class women were expected to be charming, witty, interested in the world and its doings, but not scholars. The majority of the aristocratic ladies in Molière's own audience probably took this view and shared the opinion of the men, that 'learned ladies' and their gatherings were fools, fit targets for the pedants, charlatans and other confidence-tricksters who preyed on them. In particular, they would have found bizarre the belief of Philaminte, Bélise and Armande in this play, that there is a gulf between the mind and the emotions, and that it is possible to repress one's entire emotional nature and live by mind alone.

As always, Molière kept his plot extremely simple. His interest was in social and personal satire, in what drives his characters and in the ways they interact. At the simplest level are his send-ups of intellectual pretension. Like many comedians before and since, he creates an imaginary world in which 'intellectual' discourse consists of discussing absurd theories (such as whether a phrase like 'marry gold' can be 'declined' like a verb, or that if the Earth is hit by a comet it will shatter like glass) in pompous phrases larded with as much Latin and Greek as possible. If in doubt, drop in the names of a few dead writers: Plato, Horace and Vaugelas will win you every argument. This kind of discussion, as formal in its way as modern debates or law-court proceedings, had been fashionable in ancient Greece and Rome as a way of training schoolchildren to think and express themselves logically; the 'learned ladies' extend it into an obsessive way of life, excluding all other kinds of thought or feeling.

Just as the 'learned' characters are given sterile obsessions and pedantic language, so Molière characterises the 'sensual' characters with wit, irony and emotional warmth. Chrysale's mixture of amusement and ironical self-assertion is like Mr Bennet's in *Pride and Prejudice*. Clitandre, the young lover, is appropriately eager and passionate, the incarnation of romantic gush and rush. Ariste is wry and detached, and the servants (notably Martine, the kitchen-maid dismissed by Philaminte for talking like a normal person) are warm and natural, among the most sympathetic characters in the play.

Molière reserves his most savage satire for the poet and humbug Trissotin. Trissotin is convinced that his own verses (ludicrous examples of which he recites) are as dazzling as everyone else's are preposterous. At first, his flattery of Philaminte and the others seems no more than empty-headed, pseudo-intellectual fawning. But then Ariste points out that he's doing it for a deeper reason, to win Henriette's hand in marriage and so make his fortune, and the fool turns into the villain before our eyes. And for Molière's audiences there was more. During the scandals which had followed *The School for Wives* and *Tartuffe* a few years earlier, one of his principal attackers had been a vitriol-tongued cleric, Abbé Cotin, whose assaults were as bigoted and offensive as they were brainless. At the time, Molière had responded by lampooning Cotin in such plays as *The Versailles Impromptu* and *The Critique of the School for Wives*. Now, preparing *The Learned Ladies*, he toyed with the idea of calling his foolish poet Tricotin (that is, in alchemical terms, 'distilled essence of Cotin'), but settled in the end for Trissotin. Trissotin's Act Three sonnet, 'To Princess Uranie on her Fever' parodies the 'Sonnet to Mademoiselle de Longueville, on her Quartan Ague' from Cotin's *Gallant Works* of 1659, and Trissotin's epigram 'On a Carriage the Colour of Amaranth Given to a Lady, the Friend of the Author', parodies Cotin's 'Madrigal: on an Amaranth-Coloured Carriage Bought for a Lady', from the same collection. Compared with earlier fireworks between the two men, this satire is gentle, but it must have added spice for an original audience well aware of one of the most juicy court scandals of the previous ten years.

The Learned Ladies played for a couple of dozen performances (a successful 'run' for court plays at the time) and attracted none of the hostility and scandal of Molière's more contentious works. But after the Easter break and the different court festivities of summer 1672, it was not revived. Molière was already working on his next (and, as it turned out, last) play, *The Hypochondriac*, and *The Learned Ladies* was not performed again in his lifetime. The bluestocking fashion which it satirised also dwindled, and this may account for the play's subsequent 200-year neglect: it was neither revived in France nor favoured abroad until it entered the repertory of the Comédie-Française in the 1920s, and also attracted the attention of some notable translators (most recently in English, Richard Wilbur in the US and Ranjit Bolt in Britain). It has never been as popular as Molière's other mature masterpieces – and this is regrettable, since despite the apparent limitation of its theme the play contains some of his subtlest characterisation and most pungent irony, and, in the characters of Philaminte and Trissotin, comic monsters to equal any in his output.

Molière in English

English-speaking writers have always been wary of Molière. Of all great comic writers, only Aristophanes has seemed so difficult to accommodate to another culture and a different language. The stature of Molière's plays, and his verse comedies in particular, is acknowledged, and endlessly described and dissected in academic works, but it can be hard to 'realise' in the theatre or on the page. The problem is not what the plays say – their characters and themes are universal, and Molière's genius is perfectly obvious, both as a commentator on human follies and as an inspirer of laughter. It is the way they say it. Read the wrong way, the verse plays can seem no more than parades of style for its own sake, self-conscious and sterile. (The same problem has slowed down English-speaking appreciation of the tragedies of Racine and Corneille. In fact, lacking the relief of laughter, their recognition still lags well behind Molière's.)

The problem is that rhyming couplets have an entirely different cultural resonance in French and English. Since the late sixteenth century in England, they have featured in the work of a few satirists of the first rank (Pope, say, or Byron), but have otherwise been associated with such less grand literary endeavours as the words of Gilbert and Sullivan operettas, lyric poetry, song-lyrics and doggerel. On the stage, their principal manifestation is in Christmas pantomime. In all these works, the regular rhythms and the rhymes have an effect of closure. Anticipation is aroused by the first line of the couplet, and fulfilled by the second; the effect is brilliant but short-winded. Onstage, the entertainment proceeds in jerks and starts, the rhymes acting like the verbal equivalent of a succession of sight-gags in physical slapstick. In French drama, by contrast, rhythm and rhyme have none of this corseting effect; they sound no more artificial, and impose no more limitations, than does blank verse in Shakespearean English. Only inept writers hide inside the regularity of the structure; authors like Molière and Racine think in emotional and philosophical paragraphs which over-ride it, and part of the attraction for both performers and audience is the constant syncopation, or 'pull', between freedom of thought and formality of medium. The analogy is not with formal 'classical' music – some critics have (wrongly) compared Molière's verse plays with Bach fugues or Haydn symphonies – but with traditional jazz, where the effect depends on the interplay between the basic structure of the piece, a series of chords and melodic phrases familiar to the audience, and the individual and unexpected ways performers 'riff' on it.

After the Restoration of Charles II, when the English court set out to ape all things French, Molière was popular in English adaptation, and writers such as Dryden, Shadwell, Otway and Wycherley made versions of his plays or borrowed favourite ideas and scenes. Some of their versions were in prose, but those in rhymed verse already showed the English tendency to rhyme for effect rather than in passing and made Molière seem stilted and dandyish. In the early eighteenth century he dropped out of fashion in Britain. A few writers still adapted occasional plays (Colley Cibber's *The Non-Juror* is an excellent version of *Tartuffe*), and the first complete English translation (by H. Baker and J. Miller) was published in 1739. But changes in theatre fashion left him high and dry onstage for nearly two centuries: writing in the 1890s, Shaw called Molière's *Don Juan* 'this great play' but dismissed the rest of his work as 'posturing'.

In the twentieth century, determined attempts to revive and stage the plays, both in Britain and the US, led to gradual re-emergence. Important milestones were complete translations by A.R. Waller in the 1910s-1920s (his *Learned Ladies* is the basis for the 1996 RSC adaptation published here) and by Curtis Hidden Page in the 1920s; the Gaelic-inflected adaptations made by Lady Gregory in the 1920s and known collectively as *The Kiltartan Molière;* and notable versions of single plays which reached the popular stage, one of the first of which was Somerset Maugham's *The Perfect Gentleman*, as early as 1913. In the 1950s and beyond Molière has once again found his place, with translations by such writers as John Wood, Richard Wilbur and Ranjit Bolt and a host of adaptations, including those of Neil Bartlett, Tony Harrison and Martin Crimp.

All these translations and versions differ wildly in their approach to the 'problem' of registering Molière's verse style in English. One method has been to translate them into English rhymed couplets, tackling the 'closure' problem head-on not by softening it but by drawing attention to it, making the rhymes as dazzling and ear-catching as possible. Richard Wilbur's and Ranjit Bolt's translations, in particular, are technical firework-displays, comic verse of a quality unequalled since W.S. Gilbert (but more consistent and funnier). Other translators go for 'softer' rhymes (Donald Frame), or abandon rhymes altogether (Miles Malleson). I myself have experimented with a form of free verse (inspired by Cole Porter's song-lyrics), multiply-rhymed but placing the rhymes for emotional rather than structural effect.

A.R. Waller belongs to yet another tradition. His translation was made for a bilingual edition, and is scrupulously accurate to Molière's meaning. When it came to style, he took a completely different path from those who sought to replicate Molière's verse-structures in English. In the debate, current in the 1910s, about rendering 'style' in foreign plays, some maintained that the best approach for a translator was to find a model in English literature which seemed to parallel the foreign style, and then imitate it.

In the case of Molière's 'high-style' comedy, the best English equivalent was thought to be Sheridan – and Waller set out consciously to produce, in his versions of *The Learned Ladies* and the other verse comedies, the sort of plays Sheridan might have written using Molière's themes and dialogue. Although he was no Sheridan, the result is fascinating. Using the language of English 'high-style' comedy sets Molière free. We cease to concentrate on manner, and discover instead depth of characterisation, pointful social satire and a wealth of relationships. In this play, few translations better catch the interplay between Philaminte and Martine or Armande, Bélise and Philaminte, the character of Henriette or Chrysale's endearing benignity. In fact, by putting himself in the background, Waller lets us see other aspects of Molière – and they are at least as interesting, and maybe as satisfying, as stylistic fireworks.

Original Staging

The Learned Ladies was first performed, before King and court, by the Troupe du Roi at the Théâtre du Palais-Royal on 11 March 1672. Molière himself played Chrysale, and his daughter Armande took the part of Henriette. La Grange (Molière's Don Juan in 1665) played Clitandre, and the chief bluestocking Philaminte was impersonated by Hubert, a male travesty actor who specialised in playing elderly females. The performance was given in the Théâtre du Palais-Royal, and the play was a huge success.

The Théâtre du Palais-Royal, built originally for Cardinal Richelieu, had been given to the King on Richelieu's death in 1642 and was used by Molière and his company from 1660 onwards. (It later became an Academy of Music, was burned down in 1763, rebuilt several times and, from 1799 onwards, was – and is – the Comédie-Française.) Richelieu's theatre, created from an original indoor tennis-court, was a large room, long and narrow. Its floor rose in a series of shallow steps, on which chairs were placed for the audience. At each side were balconies, also with audience seats. All in all, there was room for some 600 spectators. The stage was a raised platform at one end, with an ornate flight of steps leading down to the theatre floor. Scenery was painted on boards and canvas 'flats' set in position and removed by assistants (and 'flown' on a system of pulleys installed when the theatre was modernised in 1671). Attendants also saw to the placing or removal of props and furniture, in full view of the audience. When the stage was set, the actors strode on to it, struck attitudes and began to speak. In tragedy, the poses were statuesque (often modelled on famous artworks) and the delivery was ponderous and pompous. In comedy static dialogue was enlivened by 'business'. In some plays this was built into the script: examples are the scenes with Alain and Georgette in *School for Wives* or between Argan and the quack doctors in *The Hypochondriac*. But even in plays like *The Learned Ladies*, where the comedy is mainly verbal, it is hard to imagine such seasoned farce-performers as Molière and Hubert eschewing physical comedy entirely.

A main difference between theatre in Molière's time and today was the behaviour of the audience. The whole theatre, not just the stage, was brightly lit (by a huge central candelabrum whose hundreds of candles were ceremonially lit at the start of the performance, just before the arrival of the King and his principal courtiers, and equally solemnly snuffed at the end). The audience was there to be seen, as well as to see. Although when the King himself was present their behaviour was fairly decorous, at other times they talked, ate, played cards, flirted and occasionally even duelled while the plays were in progress. Some stood on the theatre floor, others sat on specially-brought seats – the higher a person's social rank, the more ornate their 'chaise' – and a group of (highly vocal) amateur critics sometimes took their seats on the stage or its steps themselves. (This practice, reminiscent of what happened in Shakespeare's theatres, and seeming intrusive to us today, was a major part of the audience's enjoyment even of plays as formally constructed as *The Learned Ladies*: one imagines spirited dialogue between wits and hecklers on the one hand and

Molière and his actors on the other.) Evidence suggests that particularly well-turned speeches or passages of dialogue were applauded, and that the action stopped dead while the actors took bows for them, and even sometimes repeated them.

Kenneth McLeish, 1996

For Further Reading

Although there are shelvesful of excellent academic books on Molière, works for the general reader are few and far between. The best 'biographies' are not non-fiction but a play, Bulgakov's *Molière*, and a novel, Béatrix Dussane's *An Actor Named Molière* (first published in English in 1937, but still vivid and particularly fascinating for the way it recreates the theatre-conditions of Molière's touring and court life). Among academic books, the most accessible is P.H. Nurse, *Molière and the Comic Spirit*. W.G. Moore, *Molière, a New Criticism* (1949) is the standard academic critical work, and Martin Turnell, *The Classical Moment* (1947) is a combined examination of the work of Molière, Corneille and Racine.

An alternative to books is Ariane Mnouchkine's 1986 film *Molière* (Proserpine Editions, available on video). Some scholars and purists disdain its imaginative, sometimes fanciful approach, but it gives an often moving account of Molière's life and some engrossing reconstructions of 17th-century French performances.

Molière: Key Dates

THE LEARNED LADIES

Dramatis Personae

CHRYSALE, *a well-to-do citizen (bon bourgeois)*
PHILAMINTE, *Chrysale's wife*
ARMANDE, *Chrysale and Philaminte's daughter*
HENRIETTE, *Chrysale and Philaminte's daughter*
ARISTE, *Chrysale's brother*
BÉLISE, *Chrysale's sister*
CLITANDRE, *Henriette's lover*
TRISSOTIN, *a fine wit*
VADIUS, *a scholar*
MARTINE, *kitchenmaid*
L'ÉPINE, *page-boy*
JULIEN, *Vadius's valet*
THE NOTARY

The Scene is in Paris

ACT ONE

Scene i

ARMANDE, HENRIETTE.

ARMANDE. So, sister? You want to change the sweet-sounding and delightful name of maiden and look forward to marriage with a joyful heart? Is that the vulgar notion you have in your head?

HENRIETTE. Yes, sister.

ARMANDE. Ah! That 'yes' is insufferable; who could listen to it without disgust?

HENRIETTE. What is there in marriage, sister, that makes you . . . ?

ARMANDE. Ah, good God! Fie!

HENRIETTE. What?

ARMANDE. Ah, fie! I tell you. Can you not conceive how disgusting to one's feelings is the very mention of the word? Think what shocking thoughts it brings to mind! Into what dirty paths it drags one's ideas! Do you not shudder at it? Can you persuade yourself, sister, to accept the consequences the word implies?

HENRIETTE. When I consider the consequences this word calls to mind, I see a husband, children, a home, and, when I think of those, I see nothing to shock the mind or cause one to shudder.

ARMANDE. Good Heavens! Can such ties attract you?

HENRIETTE. What can I do better, at my age, than bind myself in the ties of wedlock to a man whom I love and who loves one in return? From such a tender union flow the delights of an innocent life. Are there no attractions in such a union, if the pair be well matched?

ARMANDE. Good gracious, on what a low plane does your intellect work! What a poor figure in life you will cut if you wrap yourself up in household concerns, and never have a glimpse of any more stirring pleasures than are to be found in an idolised husband and brats of children! Leave such contemptible amusements to common people and vulgar persons. Raise your hopes to loftier amibitions, try to cultivate a taste for the noblest accomplishments, and, looking with scorn upon things of the senses and of matter, give yourself up entirely, as we do, to intellectual pursuits. You have before your eyes the example of your mother, who is reverenced far and wide for her learning: endeavour, as I do, to show yourself her daughter, aspire to those enlightened qualities which our family possesses and cultivate a sensibility to the exquisite charms that the love of study sheds over the heart; instead of being a bond slave to the dictates of a man, unite yourself, sister, in marriage with philosophy, which raises us above the whole human race and gives supreme sovereignty to the reason, subjugating to its laws the animal instincts whose gross appetites lower us to the level of the beasts. These are the sweet thoughts, the tender attachments, which should fill all life's moments; the cares to which I see so many worthy women devoted seem poor trivial things.

HENRIETTE. Heaven, whose decree is omnipotent, forms us at
   our birth for different functions; not every mind is made of the
   material from which a philosopher can be made. If you were
   created for the lofty realms to which the speculations of
   savants soar, I, sister, was made to creep on the earth and to
   confine my weak powers to the petty cares of life. Let us not
   interfere with the just orderings of Heaven, but follow the
   impulses of our own instincts: you shall take flight on the
   wings of a great philosophy, whilst I shall stay on this nether
   earth, to taste the wordly seductions of matrimony. Thus shall
   we both, in our contrary ways, imitate our mother: you on the
   side of the spirit and of noble desires, I, through the coarser
   pleasures of the senses; you, by the productions of light and
   leading, I, sister, in more material ways.

ARMANDE. When one tries to regulate one's conduct by the
   example of another, one copies the best attributes; one does
   not, sister, take as a model their trick of coughing or the way
   they spit.

HENRIETTE. But you would never have become all you boast
   of being, if my mother had only possessed spiritual qualities;
   and well it is for you, sister, that her noble genius was not
   always taken up with philosophy. I beg of you to exercise some
   indulgence towards me and allow in me those earthly qualities
   to which you owe birth. Do not, by trying to make me copy
   you, hinder the advent of some tiny savant who may wish to
   come into existence.

ARMANDE. I perceive that your mind cannot be turned from
   this mad craving after a husband; but pray let us know whom
   you intend to marry: at any rate you have not Clitandre in
   mind?

HENRIETTE. Why should I not? Is he lacking in merit? Is it a
   low choice?

ARMANDE. No; but it would be a dishonourable plan to try to snatch away another's victory; and it is a fact not unknown to the world that Clitandre has openly aspired to my hand.

HENRIETTE. Yes; but all his sighs in your direction are vain things, for you will not descend to such human weakness; you have for ever renounced matrimony, and philosophy claims all your affection: therefore, as you really have not any intentions towards Clitandre, what can it matter to you if another lays claim to him?

ARMANDE. The rule that reason sways over the senses does not necessitate the renouncement of the pleasures of adulation; one may refuse a man of merit for a husband, whom one would willingly have in one's train as an admirer.

HENRIETTE. I have not prevented him from continuing to adore at the shrine of your perfections; I only accepted the homage of his passion after your rejection of it.

ARMANDE. But, I ask you, how can you feel sure that the offer of the vows of a rejected suitor is sincere? Do you think his passion for you is so strong as to have extinguished in his heart all sighings after me?

HENRIETTE. He told me so, sister, and I readily believe him.

ARMANDE. Do not, sister, pin your faith so credulously; rather believe, when he says he has renounced me and loves you, that he does not really mean it, but deceives himself.

HENRIETTE. I do not know; but, if you are agreeable, there is a very easy way of solving the riddle: I see him coming, and he himself can, therefore, throw full light on the matter.

Scene ii

CLITANDRE, ARMANDE, HENRIETTE.

HENRIETTE. In order to relieve me of doubt my sister has suggested to me, explain yourself to us both, Clitandre; let us know your inmost thoughts, and condescend to tell us which of us is right in laying claim to your attentions.

ARMANDE. No, no: I have no desire to put your passion to the test of an avowal; I am considerate for others, and know how very embarrassing the effort must be of making such a confession in public.

CLITANDRE. No, Madam, my heart is unused to deceit, and does not feel any embarrassment in making a full confession: such an act does not throw me into any confusion. I will openly avow, with a clear and free conscience, that the tender chains which hold me, my love and passion, all tend in the same direction. The avowal cannot confuse you; indeed, as things have turned out, they are as you would have them be. Your charms fascinated me, and my tender sighs surely proved the strength of my desires; my heart offered you an eternal devotion, but your eyes did not deem the conquest they had made sufficiently worthy. Beneath their yoke I endured a hundred different slights and they ruled over my heart as contemptuous tyrants, until, weary of so many pains, I sought kinder conquerors and chains less harsh. I found them, Madam, in these eyes, and their glances will ever be precious to me; the sympathy in their looks has dried my tears, and they have not scorned to accept what you have refused. So deeply touched am I by so rare a goodness that nothing can now break my chains; I make so bold as to beseech you, Madam, not to make any effort to tempt back my passion, nor to seek to recall a heart that has resolved to die in the flames that now consume it.

ARMANDE. Ah! Who told you, Monsieur, that I had such a desire, or, indeed, that I cared for you so deeply? It is absurd of you to imagine it, and most impertinent of you to speak of it.

HENRIETTE. Come, softly, sister. Where is now that spiritual control which knows so well how to restrain animal passions in us and to put a strong curb on fits of anger?

ARMANDE. It ill becomes you to speak to me of seemliness: do you practise what you preach when you respond to a love which is offered you without leave from those who gave you being? Know that duty subjects you to their control, that you may not love except where they choose, that they have supreme authority over your affections and that it is criminal to dispose of them yourself.

HENRIETTE. I thank you for your kindness in pointing out my duty to me thus clearly; I will regulate my conduct by your precepts; and, in order to show you, sister, that I profit by them, take care, Clitandre, to strengthen your claims by the consent of those to whom I owe birth; arm yourself with legitimate authority to aspire to my hand, and give me the right to love you without fear.

CLITANDRE. I will do my utmost to gain that end. I was but waiting for your gracious permission.

ARMANDE. You triumph, sister, and, by your looks, you fancy this vexes me.

HENRIETTE. I, sister? Nothing of the kind: I know that, with you, the dictates of reason ever triumph over those of your senses; and that the lessons you have taken in wisdom raise you above any such petty feeling. Far from suspecting you of any displeasure, I believe you will condescend to use your influence in this matter on my behalf, urge his suit and, by

your suffrages, hasten the happy moment of our marriage.
I entreat you to do so; and to that end . . .

ARMANDE. Your small wit seems to find it amusing to banter:
you appear to be much elated by the offer of a rejected heart.

HENRIETTE. Rejected it may be; but it does not seem to be
greatly disliked by you; if you could snatch it back from me,
you would not refrain from stooping to do so.

ARMANDE. I will not lower myself to answer you; such idle talk
should be passed over in silence.

HENRIETTE. That is exceedingly good of you, you show us
wonderful toleration.

Scene iii

CLITANDRE, HENRIETTE.

HENRIETTE. Your sincere confession has taken her by surprise.

CLITANDRE. She deserves such blunt speech. Her haughtiness
and foolish pride quite justify my frankness. But, since you
give me leave, Madam, I will go to your father . . .

HENRIETTE. It would be safer to win over my mother: my
father is of a very yielding disposition, but little reliance can be
felt that he will carry out what he consents to do. Heaven has
endowed him with a gentle nature that submits itself first to
the wishes of his wife; she is the ruler and she lays down the
law with no uncertain voice when she has made up her mind.
I must confess I wish you were a little more amiable towards

her and towards my aunt; it would flatter them and cause them to look with kindlier eyes on you.

CLITANDRE. I am too sincere by nature ever to flatter even your sister in respect of characteristics that resemble theirs. Learned ladies are not to my taste. I like a woman to have some knowledge of all questions; but I have no patience with the detestable passion of wishing to be learned for the sake of being thought so; I would rather she at times feigned to be ignorant, when questioned, of things she knows; in short, I would rather she concealed her knowledge, and possessed it without wishing people to know that she did, without quoting authors, without using pedantic expressions, or drawing attention to her cleverness on the slightest pretext. I respect your mother greatly; but I cannot at all approve of her fancies or re-echo her sentiments when she offers incense to her intellectual idol. Her Monsieur Trissotin irritates and bores me, it angers me to see her respect such a man, to see her regard him as one of the number of great and worthy writers, a fool whose scribblings everybody derides, a pedant whose liberal pen furnishes all the shops with wrapping-up paper.

HENRIETTE. My taste and opinion agree with yours; I, too, find his writings and his conversations wearisome; but, since he has great influence with my mother, you must make yourself somewhat more compliant. A lover must pay court to the people with whom his love lives, and he must try to win favour from all; in order that no one may be against him, he must seek to ingratiate himself even with the house-dog.

CLITANDRE. Yes, you are right; but Monsieur Trissotin raises in me an overmastering dislike towards him from the very bottom of my heart. I cannot consent to dishonour myself and gain his favour by praising his works; it was through these he was first brought to my notice, and I was acquainted with them before I saw him. I discovered, in the trash of his writings, the same qualities that he displays everywhere in his pedantic person: the everlasting pride of his self-conceit, that hidebound good opinion of himself, that indolent air of supreme confidence, which makes him at all times self-satisfied, which makes him smirk so incessantly at his own merit, which gives him a good opinion of everything he writes, and provides him with a reputation which he would not exchange for all the honours of a successful general.

HENRIETTE. Your sight must be keen, to see all that.

CLITANDRE. I even depicted his face to myself. I saw by the verses that he flung at our heads of what sort of stuff the poet was made; and I guessed all his features so accurately that, meeting a man one day in the Palais, I wagered that it was Trissotin in person, and I found, indeed, that I had made a good bet.

HENRIETTE. I don't believe you!

CLITANDRE. I am telling you the very truth. But I see your aunt. Please permit me to tell her our secret now, win her good graces and so influence your mother.

Scene iv

CLITANDRE, BÉLISE.

CLITANDRE. Pray allow me a few words with you, Madam, and let a lover seize this fortunate opportunity to declare to you his sincere devotion . . .

BÉLISE. Ah! Softly, refrain from laying bare your heart to me. If I have placed you among the ranks of my admirers, let it be enough that your eyes alone interpret your passion and do not explain to me in any other language aspirations which I look upon as insulting. Love me, sigh for me, rend your soul for my charms, but do not permit me to know it. I can shut my eyes to your secret passion, so long as you keep to mute expressions; but if the lips desire to meddle in the matter, you must be banished from my sight for ever.

CLITANDRE. Do not be alarmed by the desires of my heart, Madam: Henriette is the person who charms me, and I earnestly solicit your good offices in aid of the love her beauty has inspired in me.

BÉLISE. Ah! I must confess your subterfuge is very clever: so subtle an evasion deserves praise; I never met a more ingenious device in all the novels I have read.

CLITANDRE. Madam, this is no turn of wit, it is a genuine avowal of my real feelings. Heaven has attached my heart to the charms of Henriette by ties of an unchangeable devotion; Henriette holds me under her gracious sway, and to marry Henriette is the height of my ambitions: you can do much in aid of this, and all I ask is that you will condescend to favour my suit.

BÉLISE. I see where your demand so insidiously tends and I understand whom you intend me to understand by that name. The metaphor is clever, and, in order that I may not depart from the figure of speech by answering as my heart prompts me to do, I will reply that Henriette is averse to wedlock, and that you must consume your heart out for her without claiming aught in return.

CLITANDRE. Ah! Madam, what is the good of distorted language: why do you persist in believing what is not?

BÉLISE. Good Heavens! Do not be so ceremonious. Cease to deny what your looks have often made me understand. Suffice it that I am content with the subterfuge thus adroitly suggested by your passion, and that, underneath the figure of speech which respect compels you to use, I am quite willing to suffer your homage, provided your transports are inspired by honour, and you offer none but the purest sacrifices on my altar.

CLITANDRE. But . . .

BÉLISE. Farewell: this ought to suffice you for the present; I have said more than I intended to say to you.

CLITANDRE. But your mistake . . .

BÉLISE. Stop, I am put to the blush, my modesty has already had much to bear.

CLITANDRE. I will be hanged if I love you; and sensible . . .

BÉLISE. No, no, I will not hear anything more.

CLITANDRE. To the deuce with the silly woman and her hallucinations! Did ever any one see the like of such idiocy? I will put this affair in the hands of some one else and take the advice of some sensible person.

ACT II

Scene i

ARISTE.

ARISTE. Yes, I will bring you the answer as soon as possible;
I will urge, I will insist, I will do all I can. How much a lover
has to say that could be put in one word! And how impatient
he is for what he desires! Never . . .

Scene ii

CHRYSALE, ARISTE.

ARISTE. Ah! God protect you, brother!

CHRYSALE. And you too, brother.

ARISTE. Do you know what brings me here?

CHRYSALE. No; but I am ready to hear it as soon as you like.

ARISTE. You have known Clitandre a long while?

CHRYSALE. Certainly, I often see him at our house.

ARISTE. What is your opinion of him, brother?

CHRYSALE. I think he is a man of honour, of wit, of courage and of uprightness; I know few people who are of equal merit.

ARISTE. A certain desire of his brings me here, and I am delighted you think so highly of him.

CHRYSALE. I became acquainted with his late father when I was travelling to Rome.

ARISTE. Very good.

CHRYSALE. He was, brother, a most excellent gentleman.

ARISTE. So I have heard.

CHRYSALE. We were but twenty-eight at that time and, upon my word, we were a couple of gay young sparks.

ARISTE. I well believe it.

CHRYSALE. We were much smitten with the Roman ladies, and our pranks were the talk of the whole place: we caused many jealous hearts.

ARISTE. Nothing could be better. But let us now turn to the subject which brings me here.

Scene iii

BÉLISE, CHRYSALE, ARISTE.

ARISTE. Clitandre deputes me to speak to you on his behalf; his heart is smitten with the charms of Henriette.

CHRYSALE. What! Of my daughter?

ARISTE. Yes, Clitandre is enraptured with her. I never saw a lover more smitten.

BÉLISE. No, no: I hear what you say. You do not know the true story, the matter is not what you believe it to be.

ARISTE. How so, sister?

BÉLISE. Clitandre is throwing dust in your eyes, it is someone else with whom he is in love.

ARISTE. You are joking. Is it not Henriette whom he loves?

BÉLISE. No, I am sure it is not.

ARISTE. He told me so himself.

BÉLISE. Ah! Yes!

ARISTE. I am here as you see, sister, commissioned by him to ask her this very day from her father.

BÉLISE. That is all very well.

ARISTE. He is so deeply in love that he has urged me to hasten the completion of his alliance.

BÉLISE. Better and better. He could not have employed more gallant deceit. Between ourselves, Henriette is a pretext – a cleverly devised screen, a device, brother, to hide other affections, to which I have the clue. I am quite willing to disabuse you both of your error.

ARISTE. But, since you know so many things, sister, tell us, if you please, who is the object of his love.

BÉLISE. You really wish to know?

ARISTE. Yes. Who is it?

BÉLISE. It is I.

ARISTE. You?

BÉLISE. I, myself.

ARISTE. Ho, ho, sister.

BÉLISE. What do you mean by your 'Ho! ho!'? What is there astonishing in what I have said? I am good-looking enough, I think, to be able to say that I have more than one heart under subjection to my empire; Dorante, Damis, Cleonte and Lycidas are sufficient evidence that I possess charms.

ARISTE. Those gentlemen love you?

BÉLISE. Yes, with all their hearts.

ARISTE. They have told you so?

BÉLISE. No one has taken such liberty; they have hitherto shown me too deep a reverence ever to have said a word of their love; but their mute interpreters have all done their part in offering me their hearts, and confessing their allegiance.

ARISTE. We hardly ever see Damis inside the house.

BÉLISE. That is to show me more humble respect.

ARISTE. Dorante insults you everywhere with sarcastic phrases.

BÉLISE. They are the ravings of his mad jealousy.

ARISTE. Cleonte and Lycidas have both married.

BÉLISE. That is because I reduced their passion to a state of despair.

ARISTE. Really, sister, these are simply chimeras.

CHRYSALE. You ought to rid yourself of these fancies.

BÉLISE. Ah, fancies! Fancies they call them! I fancy things! Truly, to call them fancies is quite excellent! I rejoice heartily in my fancies, dear brothers, I was not aware I had any fancies.

Scene iv

CHRYSALE, ARISTE.

CHRYSALE. Our sister is certainly mad.

ARISTE. It grows upon her every day. But, let us once more resume our conversation. Clitandre asks you for Henriette as his wife: what answer should be given to his suit?

CHRYSALE. Need you ask? I consent with all my heart, and look upon the alliance as a great honour.

ARISTE. You are aware he is not overburdened with wealth, that . . .

CHRYSALE. It is a matter of no importance; he is rich in virtue, which is of more value than wealth, and we must bear in mind that his father and I were one in spirit, though two in body.

ARISTE. Let us speak to your wife and try to make her favourable . . .

CHRYSALE. It is enough: I accept him for a son-in-law.

ARISTE. Yes; but, brother, in order to strengthen your consent, it would not be amiss to have her approval. Let us go . . .

CHRYSALE. You are jesting? It is unnecessary; I will answer for my wife, and take the business upon myself.

ARISTE. But . . .

CHRYSALE. Leave it to me, I say, and have no fear: I will go at
    once and prepare her for the news.

ARISTE. Good. I will go and sound your Henriette on the
    matter, and I will return to learn . . .

CHRYSALE. It is a foregone conclusion, I will go immediately to
    talk to my wife about it.

Scene v

MARTINE, CHRYSALE.

MARTINE. Typical! The saying is true: one rule for the rich;
    one rule for the poor. To be born into service is no great
    blessing, I can tell you.

CHRYSALE. What is it? What is the matter with you, Martine?

MARTINE. The matter with me?

CHRYSALE. Yes.

MARTINE. I have just had notice to quit, Monsieur.

CHRYSALE. Notice to quit!

MARTINE. Yes, Madam has turned me away.

CHRYSALE. I do not understand this. Why?

MARTINE. She threatens, if I do not leave, to give me a good
    thrashing.

CHRYSALE. No, you shall stay: I am satisfied with you. My wife is often a little hot tempered, and I do not wish . . .

Scene vi

PHILAMINTE, BÉLISE, CHRYSALE, MARTINE.

PHILAMINTE. What? You here still, you jade? Quick, out you go, slut; come, out of the house, and never let me set eyes on you again.

CHRYSALE. Gently.

PHILAMINTE. No, there is an end of it.

CHRYSALE. Eh!

PHILAMINTE. I intend her to go.

CHRYSALE. But what has she done to be treated in this manner?

PHILAMINTE. What? You support her?

CHRYSALE. By no means.

PHILAMINTE. Do you take her part against me?

CHRYSALE. Good gracious! No; I only ask what she has done.

PHILAMINTE. Should I be likely to dismiss her without just cause?

CHRYSALE. I do not say that; but our servants must . . .

PHILAMINTE. No; she shall go, I tell you, out of the house.

CHRYSALE. Ah! Well! Yes: no one wants to oppose you.

PHILAMINTE. I will not be opposed.

CHRYSALE. Agreed.

PHILAMINTE. And if you were a reasonable husband you would agree with me.

CHRYSALE. So I do. Indeed, my wife does right to send you away, you jade, your crime deserves no pardon.

MARTINE. But what have I done?

CHRYSALE. For my life I don't know.

PHILAMINTE. She is still in a mood to think lightly of her guilt.

CHRYSALE. Has she made you angry by breaking a mirror or some china?

PHILAMINTE. Do you imagine I should be angry over such a trifling fault as that?

CHRYSALE. You mean it is something much worse?

PHILAMINTE. Of course. Am I an unreasonable woman?

CHRYSALE. Has she been careless enough to allow a ewer or a piece of plate to be stolen?

PHILAMINTE. That would be nothing.

CHRYSALE. Oh! Oh! The deuce, my good woman! What? Have you detected her in dishonesty?

PHILAMINTE. It is worse than any of these.

CHRYSALE. Worse than any of these?

PHILAMINTE. Worse.

CHRYSALE. What the deuce, wench! Hey! Has she committed . . .

PHILAMINTE. She has been guilty of the unparalleled impudence of shocking my ears after thirty lessons, by the impropriety of using a split infinitive!

CHRYSALE. Is that all?

PHILAMINTE. What? In spite of our remonstrances, always to be undermining grammar, the foundation of all sciences, which controls even kings, and makes them obey its laws with a high hand?

CHRYSALE. I thought she was guilty of the greatest iniquity.

PHILAMINTE. What? You do not consider her crime unpardonable?

CHRYSALE. Certainly.

PHILAMINTE. I should like to see you pardon her.

CHRYSALE. I have no such intention.

BÉLISE. It is really deplorable: she destroys all construction and all the laws of language which she has been taught a hundred times.

MARTINE. All that you preach is no doubt well and good, but I shall never learn how to talk your jargon.

PHILAMINTE. Impudent girl, to call a language jargon that is founded on reason and refined manners!

MARTINE. To make oneself understood is good enough language for me; all your fine sayings don't do me no good.

PHILAMINTE. Just listen! There goes another example of her style. *Don't do me no good!*

BÉLISE. O brainless idiot! Can you not learn to speak properly
    after all the pains I have incessantly taken? To use *don't* and *no*
    is a redundancy, and is, as I have told you, a double negative.

MARTINE. Good 'Eavens! I were not eddicated like you, I talks
    just the same as other folks like me talk.

PHILAMINTE. Oh! It is unbearable!

BÉLISE. What a horrible solecism!

PHILAMINTE. It is enough to break the drum of a sensitive ear.

BÉLISE. I think your intellect must be very dense. *I* is but
    singular, while *were* is plural. Will you offend against grammar
    all your life?

MARTINE. Who said anything about offending Grandma? Or
    Grandpa for that matter?

PHILAMINTE. Oh, Heavens!

BÉLISE. *Grammar* is taken in the wrong sense by you; I have told
    you before where the word comes from.

MARTINE. Goodness me! Whether it comes from Chaillot or
    Hauteuil or Pontoise, it is all the same to me.

BÉLISE. What a clodhopping wench! Grammar teaches us the
    laws of the verb and of the nominative, as well as the adjective
    and its relation to the substantive.

MARTINE. All I can say, Madam, is, that I don't know these
    people.

PHILAMINTE. What martyrdom!

BÉLISE. They are the names of words, and one has to consider
    how they should be made to agree together.

MARTINE. What does it matter whether they agree or tear each other to pieces?

PHILAMINTE (*to her sister*). Oh! Heavens! Put an end to this discussion. (*To her husband.*) So, will you not send her away?

CHRYSALE. Yes, yes. I must yield to her caprice. Go! Do not irritate her; just retire, Martine.

PHILAMINTE. What? Are you afraid to offend the hussy? You speak to her as though you were afraid of her.

CHRYSALE. I? Nothing of the kind. Leave this house! Go away, my lass.

Scene vii

PHILAMINTE, CHRYSALE, BÉLISE.

CHRYSALE. You have your way, she has now gone; but I do not at all approve of such a dismissal. She is a girl who does her work very well, and yet you send her packing for a mere trifle.

PHILAMINTE. Do you want me to have her always in my service, incessantly to have my ear put to torture? To hear her break every law of custom and reason by a barbarous hotchpotch of errors of speech, of mutilated words, linked together at intervals by proverbs picked up in the gutters of the market-place?

BÉLISE. True, it makes one feel hot all over to have to endure listening to her way of speaking: she rends Vaugelas to pieces

every day of her life; the smallest defects of her coarse mind
are either a pleonasm or cacophony.

CHRYSALE. What does it matter that she is ignorant of the laws
of Vaugelas, provided she is a good cook? Truly, I would
much rather she failed to make her nouns agree with her verbs
while washing her vegetables, and indulged in low or bad
words a hundred times over, than burn my meat or oversalt
my soup. I live by good soup, and not on fine language.
Vaugelas does not teach how to make good soup; and
Malherbe and Balzac, however learned in fine words, would
probably have turned out fools in the matter of cooking.

PHILAMINTE. How terribly shocking this coarse conversation
is! What a degradation it is to see one who calls himself a man
always stooping to material cares, instead of lifting himself up
towards immaterial things! Is this rubbishy body of ours of
sufficient importance, of sufficient value, to deserve even a
passing thought? Ought we not to put such matters far from
us?

CHRYSALE. Yes, my body is myself, and I mean to take care of
it: call it rubbish if you like, but it is rubbish that is dear to me.

BÉLISE. The body, supported by the mind, is of some
importance, brother; but, if you believe what the whole of the
learned world says, the mind ought to take precedence over
the body. Our greatest pains, our first efforts, ought to be
devoted to nourishing it with the essence of knowledge.

CHRYSALE. Good Heavens! If you contemplate nourishing
your mind, it is, if report may be credited, with very meagre
food; you have no care, no solicitude, for . . .

PHILAMINTE. Ah! *Solicitude* is a word that offends my ear; it
savours too much of a mode of speech that has passed away.

BÉLISE. True, the word is very old-fashioned.

CHRYSALE. Do you wish to hear the truth? I cannot contain myself any longer; I must give vent to my feelings; people call you fools, and it distresses me greatly . . .

PHILAMINTE. I beg your pardon?

CHRYSALE. It is to you I speak, sister. The slightest solecism in speech annoys you; but you commit strange ones in your conduct. Your everlasting books matter very little to me. Leave science to the professors in the town; and burn all this useless lumber, except a large Plutarch to press my collars in. And you would do well to get rid of that great telescope in our garret, which is enough to scare the daylights out of people. Leave off trying to find out what they are doing in the moon, and interest yourself a little more in what is going on in your own household. It is not at all seemly, for many reasons, that a woman should spend so much time in study, and know so many things. To train the minds of her children in good ways, to manage her own household, to look after her servants and to regulate her expenses economically, that ought to be her study and her philosophy. Our fathers showed common sense on this point, when they said that a woman had reached the limit of knowledge desirable if she were capable of distinguishing a doublet from a pair of breeches. Their women did not read much, but they lived excellent lives; all their learned conversation was concerned with house-keeping, and their library consisted of a thimble, thread and needles, with which to make their daughters' trousseaux. The women of our day are far from following their example: they want to scribble, and to become authors. No science is too deep for them. It is far worse in this house of mine than anywhere else in the world: the loftiest secrets are understood, and everything is known except what ought to be known; they know the motions of the moon, the polar star, Venus, Saturn and Mars, which have nothing to do with me; and this vain, far-fetched knowledge does not include an acquaintance with the methods of cooking my food, so that I am on the verge of starvation. Philosophy is the chief occupation of every one in my household, and reasoning has banished reason. My servants aspire to science to please you, and their housework is the very last thing of all they attend to; one burns my roast whilst studying history; another dreams of verse-making when I ask for a drink; in short, your example is closely followed by them, and, although I have servants, I am not served. One poor lass at least was left me, who was not corrupted by this bad atmosphere, and, behold, she is turned out with much ado because she fails to talk according to Vaugelas. I tell you, sister, all these carryings on annoy me (for it is you, as I have said, whom I am addressing). And most of all I cannot bear all your poets, especially that Monsieur Trissotin; he has made you the laughing-stock of the town with his verses. All his poems are mere twaddle; you have to cudgel your brains to think what he has said when he has done talking, and I, for one, believe his brain is a bit cracked.

PHILAMINTE. Oh! Heavens, what mean thoughts and how meanly expressed!

BÉLISE. Could there be denser wits collected together in one small anatomy! Or a mind composed of commoner clay! And to think that I am of the same blood! I hate myself with a deadly hatred for belonging to your race, and I quit the place for very shame.

Scene viii

PHILAMINTE, CHRYSALE.

PHILAMINTE. Have you still another dart to level at me?

CHRYSALE. I? No. Let us not quarrel further: it is over. We will talk of other matters. Your eldest daughter, I perceive, has some distaste for the ties of matrimony: in short, she is a philosopher. I have nothing to object to in that, she is under good management, and you have brought her up well. But her younger sister is of a very different disposition, and I think it will be well to think of choosing a husband for Henriette . . .

PHILAMINTE. I have been thinking of just that very thing, and I will tell you what I had in view. This Monsieur Trissotin, who has not the honour of being in your good books and on whose account we are made to feel like criminals, is the husband I choose as suited to her, and I am a better judge of his worth than are you. To argue the question would be superfluous, as my mind is quite made up on all points. Above all, do not say a word of this choice of a husband, as I wish to speak to your daughter about it before you. I have reasons to justify my conduct, and I shall soon find out if you have informed her.

Scene ix

ARISTE, CHRYSALE.

ARISTE. Well, well, brother? The wife has gone out, I can see you have just had a talk with her.

CHRYSALE. Yes.

ARISTE. What is the result? Shall we have Henriette? Has she consented? Is the matter settled?

CHRYSALE. Not just yet.

ARISTE. Does she refuse?

CHRYSALE. Not in the least.

ARISTE. What then?

CHRYSALE. She offers me another man as son-in-law.

ARISTE. Another man as son-in-law!

CHRYSALE. Another.

ARISTE. What is his name?

CHRYSALE. Monsieur Trissotin.

ARISTE. What? Not the Monsieur Trissotin who . . .

CHRYSALE. Who is always spouting poetry and Latin, yes.

ARISTE. You have accepted him?

CHRYSALE. I, God forbid, indeed!

ARISTE. What did you reply?

CHRYSALE. Nothing; I am very glad I did not speak, or I might have committed myself.

ARISTE. Oh, that is brilliant reasoning! A great step foward. Did you at least manage to propose Clitandre to her?

CHRYSALE. No; for when I saw she suggested another son-in-law, I thought it better to go no further.

ARISTE. Truly, your prudence is something out of the common! Are you not ashamed of your weakness? Is it possible for a man to be so weak as to allow his wife absolute power and not to dare to oppose what she has decided?

CHRYSALE. Good gracious, brother! It is easy for you to talk; you do not know how a disturbance upsets me. I dearly love rest and peace and quietness and my wife is terrible when she is in a temper. She makes a great parade of philosophic qualities, but she is none the less choleric on that account; and her strict insistence on a moral life has no effect whatever on the sharpness of her temper. If one even mildly opposes anything she has set her heart on, there is a frightful uproar for a week after. She makes me tremble when she puts on that tone; I do not know where to put myself, she is a regular dragon; and yet, in spite of her diabolical tantrums I have to call her 'my sweetheart' and 'my darling'.

ARISTE. Come, you are jesting. Between ourselves, your wife rules over you because of your own cowardice. Her power is solely based on your weakness; it is from you she takes the title of mistress. You let yourself give way to her over-bearing ways, and allow yourself to be led by the nose. What? Though you are called a man, you cannot make up your mind for once to be one? Can't you bend a woman to your wishes and pick up sufficient courage merely to say, 'I will have it so?' You shamelessly let your daughter be sacrificed to the insane ideas which have got hold of the family, and endow a silly fool with all your wealth because of six words of Latin which he splutters out before them, a pedant whom your wife apostrophises at every turn as a great wit, a fine philosopher, a man unequalled in the writing of elegant verse, but who is, as we know, a complete charlatan? Come, once more, this is a jest; your abject cowardice makes you a laughing-stock.

CHRYSALE. Yes, you are right, I see I am wrong. Come, I must brace myself up to show more courage, brother.

ARISTE. That is well said.

CHRYSALE. It is a miserable thing to let oneself be so tyrannised over by a woman.

ARISTE. True, indeed.

CHRYSALE. She has taken advantage of my gentleness.

ARISTE. Quite right.

CHRYSALE. Too much imposed upon my good-nature.

ARISTE. Undoubtedly.

CHRYSALE. And I will let her understand this very day that my daughter is my daughter, and that I am her master, so far as choosing for her a husband whom I think fit is concerned.

ARISTE. Now, that is common sense, and I am glad to hear it.

CHRYSALE. You are on Clitandre's side and know where he lives: ask him to come to me without delay, brother.

ARISTE. I will go there at once.

CHRYSALE. I have borne this long enough, I will be a man now in spite of everybody.

ACT III

Scene i

PHILAMINTE, ARMANDE, BÉLISE, TRISSOTIN, L'ÉPINE.

PHILAMINTE. Ah! Let us sit down here, to listen at ease to these verses, they should be weighed word by word.

ARMANDE. I am burning to become acquainted with them.

BÉLISE. And we are all dying for them.

PHILAMINTE. Whatever emanates from you has charms for me.

ARMANDE. There is no other delight to compare with it.

BÉLISE. It is a dainty repast offered to my ears.

PHILAMINTE. Do not tantalise our eager desires any longer.

ARMANDE. Make haste.

BÉLISE. Cease this delay and hasten our joy.

PHILAMINTE. Sacrifice your epigram on the altar of our impatience.

TRISSOTIN. Alas! It is but a new-born babe, Madam. Its fate should, assuredly, touch you, since it was in your courtyard that I was delivered of it.

PHILAMINTE. That you are its father is sufficient to endear it to me.

TRISSOTIN. Your approbation supplies it with a mother.

BÉLISE. How witty he is!

Scene ii

HENRIETTE, PHILAMINTE, ARMANDE, BÉLISE, TRISSOTIN, L'ÉPINE.

PHILAMINTE. Ho there! Why are you running away?

HENRIETTE. For fear of disturbing so sweet a conversation.

PHILAMINTE. Come nearer and join with all your ears in the pleasure of hearing marvellous things.

HENRIETTE. I know little of the beauties of people's writings; intellectual pursuits are not in my line.

PHILAMINTE. Never mind: presently I will tell you a secret, which you ought to know.

TRISSOTIN. The sciences contain nothing that can enflame you; your only concern is the science of charm.

HENRIETTE. One is as little to me as the other; I have no desire . . .

BÉLISE. Oh! Let us reflect on the new born babe, I beseech you.

PHILAMINTE. Come, foolish boy, bring chairs quickly. (*The* PAGE BOY *falls down with the chair.*) What a clumsy youth! Ought people to fall down when they have learned the equilibrium of things?

BÉLISE. Do you not see the reason why you fell, stupid boy? It was caused by your deviation from the fixed point that we call the centre of gravity.

L'ÉPINE. I saw it, Madam, when I was on the ground.

PHILAMINTE. Clumsy fellow!

TRISSOTIN. Well for him he is not made of glass.

ARMANDE. Ah! What a ready wit.

BÉLISE. It is inexhaustible.

PHILAMINTE. Now serve us up your tempting repast.

TRISSOTIN. A dish of only eight lines seems scanty fare to appease the great hunger I see before me. I think I shall do well to add to the epigram, or, rather, to the madrigal, the seasoning of a sonnet, which a certain princess thought somewhat delicate. It is seasoned throughout with Attic salt, and you will, I believe, find it passably good.

ARMANDE. I have no doubt of it.

PHILAMINTE. Let us listen at once.

BÉLISE (*interrupting him each time he tries to begin*). I feel my heart thrill beforehand; I love poetry to distraction, particularly when the verses are gallantly turned.

PHILAMINTE. If we keep on talking he cannot say anything.

TRISSOTIN. *So . . .*

BÉLISE. Silence! Niece.

TRISSOTIN. *Sonnet to the Princess Uranie on her Fever.*

> Your prudence aslumber sure must be,
> Magnificently so to sate,
> And sumptuously accommodate
> Thy enemy, most cruel to thee!

BÉLISE. Oh! What an exquisite beginning!

ARMANDE. What a graceful turn it has!

PHILAMINTE. He alone possesses the talent for easy, flowing verses!

ARMANDE. To *prudence aslumber* we must do homage.

BÉLISE. *To accommodate thy enemy* is full of charms for me.

PHILAMINTE. I love *sumptuously* and *magnificently:* these two adverbs go admirably together.

BÉLISE. Let us bend our ear to the rest.

TRISSOTIN. Your prudence aslumber sure must be,
> Magnificently so to sate,
> And sumptuously accommodate
> Thy enemy, most cruel to thee!

ARMANDE. *Prudence aslumber!*

BÉLISE. *To accommodate thy enemy!*

PHILAMINTE. *Sumptuously* and *magnificently!*

TRISSOTIN. Say what they may, th' ingrate snake expel,
> From your apartment rich and grand,
> Where insolently this hated fiend
> Doth sound alarums of your knell.

BÉLISE. Ah! Gently; let me, I pray, breathe awhile.

ARMANDE. Please give us time to admire.

PHILAMINTE. One feels an indescribable sensation thrill to the centre of one's soul as one hears these verses; it is as though one were about to faint.

ARMANDE. Say what they may, th' ingrate snake expel,
From your apartment rich and grand.

How prettily expressed is *apartment rich and grand!* And how cleverly the metaphor is chosen!

PHILAMINTE. Say what they may, th' ingrate snake expel.

Ah! What admirable taste is shown in that *say what they may.* It is, to my thinking, an invaluable phrase.

ARMANDE. I, too, am in love with *say what they may.*

BÉLISE. I agree with you, *say what they may* is very happy.

ARMANDE. I would I had written it.

BÉLISE. It is worth a whole poem.

PHILAMINTE. But do you really appreciate its fine shades as I do?

ARM. and BEL. Oh, oh!

PHILAMINTE. Say what they may, th' ingrate snake expel.

Even if people should side with the fever, do not take any notice, jeer at their chatter.

Say what they may.
Say what they may.
Say what they may.

This *say what they may* means far more than appears at first sight. I do not know whether any one else agrees with me, but I read a million different meanings in the words.

BÉLISE. It is true it says more than its brevity expresses.

PHILAMINTE. But when you wrote this delightful *say what they may*, did you yourself realise its full force? Did you yourself think of all that it says to us, and did you intend then to suffuse it with wit?

TRISSOTIN. Ah, um . . .

ARMANDE. My head is full of the *snake:* that ungrateful *snake*, despicable fever which treats people who harbour it so badly.

PHILAMINTE. In a word, both the quatrains are admirable. Pray let us come quickly to the tiercets.

ARMANDE. Ah! Please, repeat once more *say what they may*.

TRISSOTIN. Say what they may, th' ingrate snake expel.

PHIL., ARM. and BEL. *Say what they may!*

TRISSOTIN. From your apartment rich and grand.

PHIL., ARM. and BEL. *Rich and grand!*

TRISSOTIN. Where insolently this hated fiend.

PHIL., ARM. and BEL. *This hated fiend!*

TRISSOTIN. Doth sound alarums of your knell.

PHILAMINTE. *Of your knell!*

ARM. and BEL. Ah!

TRISSOTIN. What! With no respect of your high rank
Your noble blood he basely drank.

PHIL., ARM. and BEL. Ah!

TRISSOTIN. And hourly plays some wicked prank.
　　Pray heed no more the snake's demands,
　　In steamy baths then purge your glands.
　　The serpent drown with your bare hands.

PHILAMINTE. We can bear no more.

BÉLISE. We swoon.

ARMANDE. We die of ecstasy.

PHILAMINTE. It makes a thousand gentle shiverings thrill
　　through one.

ARMANDE. *Pray heed no more the snake's demands.*

BÉLISE. *In steamy baths then purge your glands.*

PHILAMINTE. *The serpent drown with your bare hands.*

　　With your own bare hands, there, you must drown the serpent.

ARMANDE. Every step in your verses reveals charming traits.

BÉLISE. Everywhere one can wander in ecstasy.

PHILAMINTE. One treads on nothing that is not beautiful.

ARMANDE. The little by-paths are strewn with roses.

TRISSOTIN. You think the sonnet then . . .

PHILAMINTE. Admirable, original; no one has ever done
　　anything so fine.

BÉLISE. What? No emotion during such a reading? You make a
　　sorry figure here, niece!

HENRIETTE. Each of us on this earth plays the part he can,
　　aunt; a talent for wit does not come for the mere wishing.

TRISSOTIN. Perhaps my verses bore you, Madam.

HENRIETTE. Not at all. I am not listening to them.

PHILAMINTE. Ah! Let us have the epigram.

TRISSOTIN. *On a Carriage the Colour of Amaranth Given to a Lady, The Friend of the Author.*

PHILAMINTE. These titles have always something original in them.

ARMANDE. Their novelty prepares one for a hundred fine flashes of wit.

TRISSOTIN. Love has so dearly sold me his curse,

BEL., ARM. and PHIL. Ah!

TRISSOTIN. It has cost me already half my purse.
    Yet when you view this beautiful coach,
    Studded with gold like a monarch's brooch,
    That all the nation it doth amaze,
    And decks with pomp my triumphal lays.

PHILAMINTE. Ah! *My lays!* See what erudition.

BÉLISE. The conceit is excellent, one in a million.

TRISSOTIN. Yet when you view this beautiful coach,
    Studded with gold like a monarch's brooch,
    That all the nation it doth amaze,
    And decks with pomp my triumphal lays.
    Call it no more an amaranth plum
    But rather the fruits of my income.

ARMANDE. Oh, oh, oh! That was totally unexpected.

PHILAMINTE. No one but he could write in such taste.

BÉLISE. *Call it no more an amaranth plum*
But rather the fruits of my income.

'Income.' We should explore this word. In come. Come.
Come in.

PHILAMINTE. I know not whether I was prepossessed in your
favour the first moment I met you, but I admire your verse
and your prose wherever I meet it.

TRISSOTIN. If you would show me something of yours I might
also have something to admire.

PHILAMINTE. I have not written anything in verse, but I have
hopes that soon I may be able to show you, confidentially,
eight chapters of the scheme of our academy. Plato merely
fringed the subject when he wrote the treatise on his Republic;
but I shall enlarge the idea to the fullest extent. I have already
sketched it out in prose on paper. Indeed, I am exceedingly
angry at the injustice people do us with regard to our
intelligence; I intend to vindicate the whole sex, to the end
that we may be raised from the unworthy status in which men
place us, wherein our talents are limited to petty careers and
the gates that lead to sublime heights are barred against us.

ARAMDE It is offering our sex too great an insult to insist that
the scope of our intelligence shall extend no further than to
judge of a petticoat or the hand of a mantle, the beauties of
lace or or a new brocade.

BÉLISE. We must rise out of this shameful position and
emancipate ourselves.

TRISSOTIN. My respect for ladies is universally known, and,
while I render homage to the brilliancy of their glances, I also
pay honour to the light of their intelligence.

PHILAMINTE. Our sex likewise does you justice in regard to these questions; but we wish to prove to certain minds, whose pride of intellect treats us with contumely, that we women, too, are furnished with knowledge; that we, like men, can hold learned meetings, conducted by better rules; it is our wish to unite what is separated elsewhere, to mix fine language with the higher sciences, to disover in nature a thousand different experiences and on every conceivable question to allow every conceivable opinion but to espouse none.

TRISSOTIN. In the matter of order, I pin my faith to Peripateticism.

PHILAMINTE. In abstract things, I love Platonism.

ARMANDE. Epicurus pleases me, for his tenets are well based.

BÉLISE. I manage to satisfy myself with the theory of atoms; but I find it difficult to suffer the notion of a vacuum, and I have a greater relish for subtile matter.

TRISSOTIN. As regards magnetic attraction, it seems to me that Descartes has much in his favour.

ARMANDE. I adore his vortices.

PHILAMINTE. And I, his falling worlds.

ARMANDE. I long to see our assembly opened, and to announce ourselves by some discovery.

TRISSOTIN. Much is expected from your quick intelligence, for nature witholds few secrets from you.

PHILAMINTE. Without flattering myself, I may say that I have already made one discovery: I have plainly seen men in the moon.

BÉLISE. I do not think I have yet seen men, but I have seen towers as plainly as I see you.

ARMANDE. We shall probe to the depths of physics, grammar, history, poetry, moral philosophy and politics.

PHILAMINTE. Moral philosophy has charms which take my fancy for it was formerly the favourite study of great minds; but I prefer the Stoics, I think nothing is finer than their ideal wise man.

ARMANDE. In a short while our rules as to language will be made known, and, in this respect, we lay claim to have made some changes. Whether from an instinctive or a well-considered antipathy, we have each of us conceived a mortal hatred towards a number of words, be they verbs or nouns, and these we mutually agree to abandon; we are preparing sentences of death against them; and we shall open our learned conferences by proscriptions of all those diverse words from which we wish to purify both prose and poetry.

PHILAMINTE. But the finest project of our academy, a noble undertaking which enchants me, a glorious design which all the finest minds of posterity will extol, is to cut off those filthy innuendoes which are the cause of scandal in the most beautiful of words, those incessant playthings of fools of every age, those loathsome commonplaces of our sorry jesters, those sources of a mass of shameless equivocations by aid of which the modesty of women is outraged.

TRISSOTIN. These are certainly admirable projects!

BÉLISE. You shall see our statutes when they are finally drawn up.

TRISSOTIN. They will none of them fail to be perfect and wise.

ARMANDE. Our laws will make us judges of each work produced; whether prose or verse, it will be subjected to the test of our laws; no one save us and our friends will have any wit; we shall try to find fault all round, so that no one will be capable of writing well but ourselves.

Scene iii

L'ÉPINE, TRISSOTIN, PHILAMINTE, BÉLISE, ARMANDE, HENRIETTE, VADIUS.

L'ÉPINE. Monsieur, there is a man here who wishes to speak to you; he is clad in black and speaks in low tones.

TRISSOTIN. It is that learned friend who has urgently intreated me to procure him the honour of your acquaintance.

PHILAMINTE. You have our full leave to introduce him. At the least let us display our wit to the best advantage. Stop! I told you plainly enough I wanted you.

HENRIETTE. What for?

PHILAMINTE. Come here, I will tell you shortly.

TRISSOTIN. This is the gentleman who is dying to know you. In introducing him to you, I have no fear of incurring the blame of admitting a barbarian into your circle, Madam; he can hold his own amongst the finest wits.

PHILAMINTE. The hand which presents him is alone a sufficient guarantee of his worth.

TRISSOTIN. He has a complete knowledge of the old authors, and knows Greek, Madam, as well as any man in France.

PHILAMINTE. Greek, O Heavens! Greek! He knows Greek, sister!

BÉLISE. Ah, niece, Greek!

ARMANDE. Greek! How delightful!

PHILAMINTE. What! Monsieur knows Greek? Ah, pray allow us for the love of Greek, Monsieur, to embrace you.

He kisses them all except HENRIETTE, *who declines.*

HENRIETTE. Excuse me, Monsieur, I do not understand Greek.

PHILAMINTE. I have a great respect for Greek books.

VADIUS. I fear the ardent desire which prompted me to pay my homage to you today, Madam, may be inconvenient, and that I have interrupted a learned discussion.

PHILAMINTE. Possessing a knowledge of Greek, Monsieur, you can never be in the way.

TRISSOTIN. Besides, he does wonders in verse as well as in prose, and, were he inclined, he could show you something.

VADIUS. It is a failing among authors to monopolise conversation with talk of their own productions, at the Palace, at the Court, in the private assemblies and at table, they never grow weary of reading their wearisome verses. Now, I am of the opinion that there is nothing sillier than to see an author going about everywhere begging for praise, and, catching the ear of his first victims, making them often enough the martyrs of his vigils. No one has ever detected this silly infatuation in me; I am at one with the Greek who, by a special decree, forbade all his learned people to give way to the unseemly eagerness of reading their own works. Here are some slight verses for young lovers, upon which I should much like to have your opinion.

TRISSOTIN. Your verses exhibit beauties that no other verses possess.

VADIUS. Venus and the Graces reign in all yours.

TRISSOTIN. You have a free style and a fine choice of words.

VADIUS. *Ethos* and *pathos* are visible throughout your works.

TRISSOTIN. We have seen some of your eclogues which, by the exquisite grace of their style, surpass those of Theocritus and Vergil.

VADIUS. Your odes have a noble, gallant and tender air, which leaves those of Horace far behind.

TRISSOTIN. Could anything be more lovely than your canzonets?

VADIUS. Could anything equal your sonnets?

TRISSOTIN. Is there anything more delightful than your little *rondeaux*?

VADIUS. Or anything so full of wit as are all your madrigals?

TRISSOTIN. You are especially good in the ballade.

VADIUS. I think you are adorable in *bouts-rimés*.

TRISSOTIN. If only France realised your worth.

VADIUS. If the age did but render proper justice to great wits.

TRISSOTIN. You would drive through the streets in a gilded coach.

VADIUS. We should see the public erecting statues to you. Hum! Here is a ballade, and I should like you frankly to . . .

TRISSOTIN. Have you seen a certain little sonnet upon the fever which attacked the princess Uranie?

VADIUS. Yes, it was read to me yesterday at an assembly.

TRISSOTIN. Do you know its author?

VADIUS. No; but I am quite well aware that, to speak truth, his sonnet is worthless.

TRISSOTIN. Many people, however, think it admirable.

VADIUS. That does not prevent it from being wretched; and, had you seen it, you would have agreed with me.

TRISSOTIN. I know I should not at all have done so on this subject; few people are capable of composing such a sonnet.

VADIUS. May Heaven preserve me from producing any like it!

TRISSOTIN. I maintain that nothing better could have been written, and my chief reason is that I am the author of it.

VADIUS. You!

TRISSOTIN. I.

VADIUS. I cannot understand this at all.

TRISSOTIN. The fact is, I was so unfortunate as to fail to please you.

VADIUS. My attention must have been wandering while I was listening, or, indeed, the reader may have spoilt the sonnet for me. But let us quit this subject and turn to my ballade.

TRISSOTIN. The ballade, to my way of thinking, is an insipid affair. It is no longer the fashion; it savours of past times.

VADIUS. Nevertheless the ballade has charms for many people.

TRISSOTIN. That does not prevent me from disliking it.

VADIUS. It is none the worse on that account.

TRISSOTIN. It has a wonderful attractions for pedants.

VADIUS. Yet we see that it does not please you.

TRISSOTIN. You foolishly attribute your qualities to others.

VADIUS. You very impertinently throw yours at me.

TRISSOTIN. Get off, you miserable dunce, you quill-driver.

VADIUS. Get off, you penny-a-liner, you disgrace to the profession.

TRISSOTIN. Get off, you second-hand book-maker, you impudent plagiarist.

VADIUS. Get off, you jumped-up pedagogue . . .

PHILAMINTE. Come! Messieurs, what are you about?

TRISSOTIN. Off and make restitution for all the shameful larcenies you are guilty of from the Greeks and Latins.

VADIUS. Off and make amends to Parnassus for murdering Horace by your verses.

TRISOTTIN Remember your book and what little stir it made.

VADIUS. And you, your publisher reduced to the workhouse.

TRISSOTIN. My fame is established; it is no use you trying to destroy it.

VADIUS. Well, well, I refer you to the critic Bol.

TRISSOTIN. I refer you to him also.

VADIUS. I have the satisfaction of knowing that he thinks more highly of me than of you: this is very evident; he gives me a slight dig, by the way, amongst other authors who are esteemed at the Palace; but he never leaves you a moment's peace in his verses; you are made the target of his arrows throughout.

TRISSOTIN. It is on that very account I hold a more honourable rank. He placed you among the herd, with all other insignificant beings, he thought one blow was enough to knock you down and he has never done you the honour of repeating it; but me he attacks singly, as a noble adversary, against whom he considers all his strength is required; his oft repeated blows, aimed everywhere at me, show that he never feels certain of victory.

VADIUS. My pen shall teach you what sort of a man I am.

TRISSOTIN. And mine shall make you recognise your master.

VADIUS. I challenge you in verse, prose, Greek and Latin.

TRISSOTIN. Very well, we meet down at Barbin's bookshop.

Scene iv

TRISSOTIN, PHILAMINTE, ARMANDE, BÉLISE, HENRIETTE.

TRISSOTIN. Do not blame my outburst of anger: I was defending your judgement, Madam, which he had the audacity to attack in the matter of the sonnet.

PHILAMINTE. I shall devote myself to a reconciliation between you. But let us talk of another affair. Come here, Henriette. For a long time my mind has been troubled because no trace of wit makes itself apparent in you, but I have found a means whereby you may have this supplied.

HENRIETTE. You take unnecessary pains on my behalf. Learned conversations are not at all in my line; I like to take life easily. It takes too much trouble to be clever in everything one says; such an ambition never enters my head. I am very well content, mother, to remain stupid; I much prefer to talk as every one else does rather than worry myself about cultured language.

PHILAMINTE. Yes, but that is what wounds me. I do not intend to endure such a disgrace from one of my own flesh and blood. Physical beauty is skin-deep, a frail ornament, a flower that fades, the splendour of a moment, whilst that of the mind is inherent and solid. I have, therefore, been searching for a long time for a method whereby you might become possessed of that beauty which the years cannot destroy, a means of inspiring you with a desire for learning, of equipping you with a knowledge of great things, in short, I have made up my mind to unite you to a man of great intellect, and that man is Monsieur, who is destined by my choice to be your husband.

HENRIETTE. My husband?

PHILAMINTE. Yes, your husband. So don't play the fool with me.

BÉLISE. I understand you: your eyes demand my consent to pledge elsewhere a heart that is mine. Go, I am quite willing. I surrender you to this bond: it is a marriage that will be the making of you.

TRISSOTIN. I cannot find words, Madam, in which to express my delight; the union with which I find myself honoured puts me . . .

HENRIETTE. All in good time, Monsieur, it is not accomplished yet; do not be in such a hurry.

PHILAMINTE. What an answer! Do you know that . . . Enough, you understand me. She shall be amenable; come let us leave her.

Scene v

HENRIETTE, ARMANDE.

ARMANDE. Our mother's provision for you is excellent, she could not have chosen a more illustrious husband.

HENRIETTE. If the choice be so fine, why not take it yourself?

ARMANDE. It is upon you, not upon me, his hand is bestowed.

HENRIETTE. I will surrender it heartily. You are my elder sister.

ARMANDE. If wedlock seemed as charming to me as it does to you, I would accept your offer with ecstasy.

HENRIETTE. If my head were as full of pedants as yours I should think him a very decent match.

ARMANDE. Although our tastes may differ in this, we ought, sister, to obey our parents: a mother has absolute power over her daughters, and in vain do you think by your resistance to . . .

Scene vi

CHRYSALE, ARISTE, CLITANDRE, HENRIETTE, ARMANDE.

CHRYSALE. Come, daughter, you must fall in with my views. Clasp hands with Monsieur, and henceforth look upon him in your heart as the man whose wife I wish you to become.

ARMANDE. On this side, sister, your inclinations are strong enough.

HENRIETTE. We must obey our parents, sister: a father has absolute power over his daughters' actions.

ARMANDE. A mother also has the right to our obedience.

CHRYSALE. What do you mean?

ARMANDE. I mean that I am much afraid my mother and you are not in agreement in this matter; it is another husband . . .

CHRYSALE. Hold your tongue, you prating baggage! Take your fill of philosophising with her, and do not meddle with my actions. Tell her my intention, and caution her well not to provoke me. You can go and do so at once.

ARISTE. Excellent: you are doing wonders.

CLITANDRE. What rapture! What joy! Ah! How sweet is my lot!

CHRYSALE. Come, take her hand and go in front of us; lead her to her chamber. Ah! What sweet caresses! My heart feels warmed at the sight of all these tender emotions; they make my old flesh young again, and bring back to remembrance thoughts of my own love affairs. Come.

ACT IV

Scene i

ARMANDE, PHILAMINTE.

ARMANDE. Yes, she did not hesitate for a moment: she made a boast of her obedience. Hardly was there time for her heart to receive permission than she surrendered it before my very eyes; she seemed less to follow the wishes of a father, than to enjoy setting at defiance the commands of a mother.

PHILAMINTE. I will soon show her to which of the two the laws of reason make her submit, and whether she shall be ruled by her father or her mother, mind or body, form or matter.

ARMANDE. They might at least have paid you the compliment of consulting you; this young gentleman behaves strangely in wanting to become your son-in-law in spite of your wishes.

PHILAMINTE. He has not yet attained his heart's desire. I thought sufficiently well of him, and I approved of your love-making; but his behaviour always displeased me. He knew, thank God, that I dabbled in authorship, and yet he never begged me to read him anything.

Scene ii

CLITANDRE, ARMANDE, PHILAMINTE.

ARMANDE. If I were you, I would not for a moment allow him to become the husband of Henriette. It would be doing me great wrong to think that I speak in this matter as an interested party, and that I feel any secret spite in my heart on account of the mean trick it is evident he has played me: the soul fortifies itself against such blows as these by the solid consolations of philosophy, which help one to rise superior to everything. But to treat you thus is enough to drive you to extremes; your honour compels you to oppose his desires. However, he is a man who would never please you. Between ourselves, I have never thought that, in his heart of hearts, he had any respect for you.

PHILAMINTE. Contemptible fool!

ARMANDE. However much your fame was talked about, he himself always praised you frigidly.

PHILAMINTE. The churl!

ARMANDE. And a score of times when I have read him your new verses he has not thought them good.

PHILAMINTE. The impertinent fellow!

ARMANDE. We were often at loggerheads about it; you would not believe how much nonsense . . .

CLITANDRE. Ah! Gently, I pray you: a little charity, Madam, or, at any rate, a little honesty. What harm have I done you? What is my offence, that you should direct your eloquence against me? Do you want to destroy me, do you take so much trouble in order to ridicule me in the eyes of people of whom I stand in need? Speak, tell me whence comes this inflamed rage? I am quite willing that Madam should judge fairly between us.

ARMANDE. If I were as angry as you think me, I should be able to show sufficient ground to justify my action: you deserve it only too well, for a first passion establishes such sacred claims upon the soul, that it is better to lose one's fortune and renounce life itself than to sacrifice at the altar of another love; nothing is more wicked than changed vows, for every unfaithful heart is a blot on morality.

CLITANDRE. Do you call that infidelity, Madam, which the pride of your heart has forced upon me? I only obey the commands it imposed upon me; and, if I offend you, it alone is the cause thereof. Your charms at first possessed my whole heart: for two years my passion burned with devoted ardour; there were no assiduous attentions, duties, respectful services that were not offered in loving sacrifice to you. But my passion, my attentions, are all as nothing to you; you ran counter to my tenderest feelings. What you refuse I offer to another. Consider, Madam, is it my fault or yours? Does my heart welcome change, or is it that you urge me to it? Can it be said that I am leaving you rather than that you are driving me away?

ARMANDE. Do you call running counter to your love, Monsieur, to deprive it of its vulgar elements, and to wish to reduce it to that purity in which the beauty of perfect love consists? Could you not keep your feeling for me clear and disentangled from the commerce of the senses? Could you not appreciate the most exquisite fascination of that union of hearts in which the body has no part? Could you only love sensuality, with all its paraphernalia of material bonds? In order to feed the fires which I kindled in your heart, had marriage to be necessary, with all that it involves? Ah! What a strange kind of love! Lofty souls are far removed from the heat of such terrestrial flames! In all their affections the senses never have part; only in spirit do their fine natures mix; all else is rejected as unworthy. It is a fire pure and clear as the celestial flames; towards it none but virtuous sighs aspire, filthy desires having no part therein; nothing impure is intermingled with its aims; it loves for love's sake, and not for anything else. All its transports are directed to the mind alone, it is unaware of the very existence of the body.

CLITANDRE. But, pray forgive me, Madam, I have the misfortune to perceive that I have a body just as well as a soul. I am conscious that it is too intimately connected with the soul to be left out of consideration: I do not understand the art of separating them. Heaven has denied to me that philosophy, and my soul and my body work together. There is nothing more beautiful, as you have said, than those purified desires, which belong only to the mind, those unions of hearts and those tender thoughts which are entirely free from the commerce of the senses. But such love is too refined for me; I am, as you are good enough to observe, somewhat coarse, I love with the whole of my nature, and I must confess that love, as it appears to me, means desire for the whole person. It is not a matter that calls for condemnation; and, without doing injustice to your noble sentiments, may I say that my method is very generally followed in the world; and that marriage is fashionable enough and is accepted so readily as a worthy and tender bond, as to have filled me with the desire of seeing myself your husband, without suspecting that the liberty of such a thought would give you cause to be offended at it.

ARMANDE. Well, well, Monsieur! Well, well! Since your sensual feelings mean to gratify themselves, without listening to me; since, to compel you to faithful devotion, you must be tied by fleshly bonds and corporeal chains, I will try, if my mother be willing, to make up my mind to consent to what you wish.

CLITANDRE. It is too late, Madam, another has taken the place; and it would be an ill return on my part to abuse the protection and wound the kind feelings which ever sheltered me against your contempt.

PHILAMINTE. But come, Monsieur, are you counting upon my consent to this other marriage which you are contemplating? And tell me, pray, if it enters into your dreams that I have another husband in view for Henriette?

CLITANDRE. Ah! Madam! Reconsider your choice, I beseech you. Pray expose me to less ignominy than to subject me to the unworthy fate of seeing myself the rival of Monsieur Trissotin. That love of culture which tells against me in your house could not set up a less noble adversary against me. There are many whom the bad taste of the time has given credit for being men of letters; but Monsieur Trissotin has not been able to deceive any one; everybody appraises his writings at their true value and, outside this house, he is known everywhere for what he is worth. I have been astonished beyond measure scores of times to see you exalt silly nonsense to the skies that you would have disowned had you been the author of it yourself.

PHILAMINTE. If you judge of him quite differently from us, it is because we see him with other eyes than do you.

Scene iii

TRISSOTIN, ARMANDE, PHILAMINTE, CLITANDRE.

TRISSOTIN. I have a great piece of news to tell you. We have had a narrow escape while sleeping, Madam. Another world passed by us and fell into our vortex; if it had run into our earth on its way, we should have been smashed to pieces like glass.

PHILAMINTE. Let us postpone this discourse to another occasion: this gentleman would see neither rhyme nor reason in it; he professes to cherish ignorance and to hate both wit and knowledge.

CLITANDRE. That statement requires some qualification. I will explain myself, Madam. I only hate knowledge and wit when they spoil people. These are things good and beautiful in themselves; but I much prefer to be in the ranks of the ignorant than to be learned in the way some people are.

TRISSOTIN. No matter what people say, I, for one, do not believe that learning can possibly spoil anything.

CLITANDRE. And I am of opinion that, in deeds as well as in words, learning is capable of making great fools.

TRISSOTIN. That is a strange paradox.

CLITANDRE. Without being very clever, it would, I think, be very easy to produce proof of what I say: if reasons failed me I am quite sure that, in any case, notable examples would not.

TRISSOTIN. You might easily cite some which would not prove a thing.

CLITANDRE. I need not travel far to discover what I seek.

TRISSOTIN. These famous examples are not visible to me.

CLITANDRE. I perceive them so plainly that they almost blind me.

TRISSOTIN. I believed hitherto that it was ignorance which made people fools and not learning.

CLITANDRE. You made a great mistake; I assure you that a learned fool is a bigger fool than an ignorant fool.

TRISSOTIN. Public opinion is opposed to your maxims, since ignoramus and fool are almost synonyms.

CLITANDRE. But if we take words in the usual way, there is a far closer alliance between pedant and fool.

TRISSOTIN. An ignoramus is folly, pure and simple.

CLITANDRE. A pedant personifies unalloyed pomposity.

TRISSOTIN. The quest for knowledge has intrinsic merit.

CLITANDRE. But when pursued by a fool it is mere fatuity.

TRISSOTIN. You must be in love with ignorance to defend it so warmly.

CLITANDRE. If ignorance has so great a fascination for me, it is only since I have become acquainted with certain scholars.

TRISSOTIN. The 'certain scholars' of whom you speak may, when better known, prove to be worth more than certain persons here present.

CLITANDRE. Yes, if those 'certain scholars' are to be believed; but certain persons might not be willing to give credit to them.

PHILAMINTE. It seems to me, Monsieur . . .

CLITANDRE. Ah! Madam, have pity: Monsieur is quite strong enough without any assistance; I have already but too formidable an assailant, and my defence is to cover my retreat.

ARMANDE. But the offensive acerbity of each retort which you . . .

CLITANDRE. Another ally; I give up the game.

PHILAMINTE. Such battles are permissible in conversation, provided no personalities be used.

CLITANDRE. But, Heavens! Nothing has been said that could offend him: he understands banter as well as any man in France; he has been pricked with many a dart, and his pride has never found aught but a cause for mockery therein.

TRISSOTIN. I am not surprised to see the part Monsieur takes in the combat I am waging. He is deeply attached to court life, and that explains everything. The court, as everybody knows, does not hold with learning; it has a certain interest in supporting ignorance, and it is as a courtier he takes up its defence.

CLITANDRE. You are very hard on the poor court: its misfortune is great, indeed, when men of learning like yourself declaim daily against it, accusing it of being the cause of all your troubles, charging it with its lack of taste, accusing it, alone, for your ill-success. Allow me to say, Monsieur Trissotin, with all the respect your name inspires, that you and your *confrères* would be better advised were you to speak of the court in more measured language; that, after all, it is not really so stupid as you gentlemen imagine; that it has the common sense to take a wider outlook; that there is good taste to be found there; and that the worldly wisdom current there is, without flattery, worth all the obscure learning of pedantry.

TRISSOTIN. We are witnesses, Monsieur, of an incarnation of its good taste.

CLITANDRE. Where, Monsieur, do you detect its bad taste?

TRISSOTIN. In this, Monsieur, that Rasius and Baldus are an honour to learning in France, that their merit is patent to

everyone and yet that it does not attract either recognition or
bounty from the court.

CLITANDRE. I see what it is that annoys you, and you forbear
to rank yourself with them, Monsieur, from modesty; leaving
you, therefore, out of the question, what do your clever
gentlemen do for the State? How do their writings render
service to it by accusing the court of callous injustice, by
complaining everywhere that it fails to bestow the favour of its
patronage on their learned selves? Their knowledge is very
necessary to France, and the court stands in great need of
their books. Three beggarly scribblers take it into their puny
heads to imagine that to be published and bound in calf makes
them important personages in the State; that they can mould
the destiny of crowns by means of their pens; that, as soon as
their productions begin to be talked about, pensions ought to
rain down upon them; that the looks of the whole universe are
centred upon them; that their reputation has spread
everywhere and that they think themselves famous prodigies
of learning, because they know what others have said before
them, because they have used their eyes and their ears for
thirty years, because they have spent nine or ten thousand
nights dabbling in Greek and Latin, and in loading their
minds with the sodden rubbish of all the old trash which is
to be found in books. These people always seem intoxicated
with their own knowledge, and their only claim to merit
consists in their possessing a wealth of importunate babble,
good for nothing, void of common sense, full of absurd
impertinence, causing them everywhere to despise wit and
knowledge.

PHILAMINTE. You wax very hot, and this burst of anger
indicates the tendencies of your nature: it is the name of rival
that excites in you . . .

Scene iv

JULIEN, TRISSOTIN, PHILAMINTE, CLITANDRE, ARMANDE.

JULIEN. The learned gentleman who has just paid you a visit, whose servant I have the honour to be, exhorts you, Madam, to read this note.

PHILAMINTE. However important the letter may be that I am desired to read, you should know, my friend, that it is rude to come and interrupt people in the midst of a conversation, and that a valet who knows how to behave should apply to the servants of the household for leave to come in.

JULIEN. I will make a note of that, Madam, in my book.

PHILAMINTE. (*reads*). *Trissotin boasts, Madam, that he will wed your daughter. I warn you that his philosophy is directed only to your wealth, and that you will do well not to conclude this marriage before you have seen the poem which I am writing against him. Whilst waiting for this portrait, wherein I mean to paint him for you in his true colours, I send you Horace, Vergil, Terence and Catullus, wherein you will find marked in the margin all the passages he has pilfered.*

PHILAMINTE (*proceeds*). As soon as the marriage on which I have set my heart is announced, a crowd of enemies arise to frustrate my virtuous efforts. Today's outburst of abuse makes it expedient for me to take action which shall confound envy, and make it feel that the effort it has made to prevent the marriage has only hastened it. Go and report all this at once to your master and tell him that, in order to show him what great store I set by his noble counsels, and how worthy of being followed I esteem them, I will this very night marry my daughter to that gentleman. You, Monsieur, as a family friend, shall be present to sign their contract: I wish you to be there. Armande, be sure you send to the Notary, and go and tell your sister all this.

ARMANDE. There is no need to warn my sister; this gentleman will take the trouble of conveying the news to her at once and of disposing her heart to rebel against you.

PHILAMINTE. We shall see who will have most power over her and whether I can reduce her to a sense of her duty. (*She goes out.*)

ARMANDE. I greatly regret, Monsieur, to see that things are not turning out quite according to your wishes.

CLITANDRE. I am going to set to work in earnest, Madam, to relieve your heart of its poignant regret.

ARMANDE. I am afraid that your efforts will not achieve a happy issue.

CLITANDRE. Perhaps you will find that your fears were groundless.

ARMANDE. I hope it may be so.

CLITANDRE. I am sure of it, and that I shall be supported by your assistance.

ARMANDE. Of course, I will serve you to the best of my power.

CLITANDRE. And for such service you may rely on my gratitude.

Scene v

CHRYSALE, ARISTE, HENRIETTE, CLITANDRE.

CLITANDRE. Without your support, Monsieur, I shall be very unhappy: your wife has rejected my addresses, and her prejudiced mind desires Trissotin for a son-in-law.

CHRYSALE. What on earth is going on in her head? Why the deuce does she want this Monsieur Trissotin?

ARISTE. Because his name has the honour of rhyming with Latin, which gives him an advantage over his rivals.

CLITANDRE. She wishes to conclude the marriage tonight.

CHRYSALE. This very night?

CLITANDRE. This very night.

CHRYSALE. And this very evening I mean to marry you both, in order to thwart her.

CLITANDRE. She has sent for the Notary, to draw up the contract.

CHRYSALE. And I am going to send for the notary to draw one up for me.

CLITANDRE. Madam is to be informed by her sister of the marriage to which they wish her to consent.

CHRYSALE. I command her with a father's authority to prepare herself for this other alliance. Ah! I will let them see whether there is to be any other master to lay down the law in my house but myself. We will return soon. Be careful to wait for us. Come, follow me, brother, and you also, son-in-law.

HENRIETTE. Alas! You must keep him always in this humour.

ARISTE. I will do everything I can to further your love-making.

CLITANDRE. However powerful the aid that is promised to my suit, my greatest hope lies in you, Madam.

HENRIETTE. You may rest assured my heart is yours.

CLITANDRE. With that assurance I cannot but be happy.

HENRIETTE. You see to what a union they mean to compel me.

CLITANDRE. So long as you are mine, I see nothing to fear.

HENRIETTE. I am going to try everything to further our earnest desires; and, if all my efforts fail to make me yours, there is a holy retreat wherein my soul can find refuge, which will save me from belonging to any one else.

CLITANDRE. May the good God spare me from ever receiving such a proof of your love!

ACT V

Scene i

HENRIETTE, TRISSOTIN.

HENRIETTE. I wish, Monsieur, to speak to you privately about
the marriage my mother has in view; I thought that, seeing
the trouble into which the house is cast, I might be able to
persuade you to listen to reason. I know you believe that my
alliance with you will bring you a well-endowed bride; but
money, by which so many people set store, is, to a true
philosopher, but a worthless allurement; and contempt of
riches and of empty display ought not to reveal itself only
in your words.

TRISSOTIN. And it is not in that respect that you charm me;
your brilliant beauty, your sweet and penetrating looks, your
grace, your bearing, are the dowry, the wealth, which have
attracted my desires and tender feelings towards you: they
are the sole riches with which I am in love.

HENRIETTE. I am very grateful to you for your generous
passion: such devoted love overwhelms me and I regret,
Monsieur, I am unable to respond to it. I esteem you as much
as it is possible to esteem another; but there is an obstacle in
the way of my loving you: a heart, you know, cannot belong
to two people, and I feel that Clitandre has made himself

master of mine. I am aware that he has much less merit than you, that I show but sorry taste in the choice of a husband, that you possess a hundred fine talents which ought to cause me to prefer you; I see clearly that I am wrong, but I cannot help it; the only effect reason has on me is to make me reproach myself for being so blind.

TRISSOTIN. The gift of your hand, to which I am permitted to aspire, will set free the heart Clitandre possesses; and I venture to presume that, by means of a thousand little attentions, I shall discover the art of making myself beloved.

HENRIETTE. No: my heart is bound by its first inclinations and cannot be touched, Monsieur, by your attentions. I venture to open my heart freely to you in this matter, and my confession contains nothing that ought to offend you. It is common knowledge that the passionate love which sets fire to hearts is not created by merit: caprice is responsible for a share in it, and often, when some one takes our fancy, we cannot tell the reason why. If we could love, Monsieur, to order, and according to the dictates of prudence, you should possess my whole heart and my affection; but we know that love is not thus controlled. Leave me, I pray you, to my blindness and do not profit by that violation of my feelings proposed to be forced upon me. An honourable man does not like to take advantage of the power parents have over us; he shrinks with repugnance from the sacrifice to him of the being he loves, and he is content only with the heart he himself has won. Refrain from urging my mother to exercise her supreme authority over me in her choice; withdraw your offer and bestow upon another the homage of a heart as inestimable as is yours.

TRISSOTIN. How can I grant your wishes? Impose upon me commands which I can fulfill. How could I cease to love you,

Madam, unless you ceased to be lovable and your heavenly charms to be no longer apparent . . .

HENRIETTE. Oh, Monsieur, cease this fooling. You have portrayed the charms of so many Irises, Philises and Amarantes, throughout your verses, to whom you vow equally intense passion . . .

TRISSOTIN. My brain speaks to those, not my heart: I am only in love with them as a poet; but the adorable Henriette I love with all my heart.

HENRIETTE. Oh! I beg of you, Monsieur . . .

TRISSOTIN. If my love offends you, the offence is not likely to cease. This passion that hitherto you have ignored has sworn to consecrate its vows to you for ever; nothing can stop its delicious ecstasy; and, should your beauty deny my passion, I can hardly decline the aid of a mother who is willing to set the seal upon a bond to me so precious; provided I obtain so delightful a happiness, provided I obtain you, it doesn't matter how.

HENRIETTE. But do you realise that you will risk more than you think by using violence to compel obedience? To speak frankly, a man who marries a woman against her wishes stands on very uncertain ground, for, if she feels constrained, she may take those means of revenge which every husband should dread.

TRISSOTIN. Such talk as that does not affect me: a wise man is prepared for all events; reason cures him of vulgar weaknesses, he rises superior to such fears, and is proof against any shadow of annoyance at things beyond his control.

HENRIETTE. Really, Monsieur, you enchant me; I had no idea philosophy could teach men to endure that particular vagary of torture. Surely, this strength of mind which seems so peculiar to you deserves to be given a far greater challenge than I can offer; you ought to find someone whose love would take ceaseless pains to put you to the test; and as, truly, I dare not consider myself capable of undertaking the task of adding to your glory, I will leave it to someone else. I venture to take the liberty of swearing that I renounce the happiness of being your wife.

TRISSOTIN. We shall soon see how matters will end – the notary is already within.

Scene ii

CHRYSALE, CLITANDRE, MARTINE, HENRIETTE.

CHRYSALE. Ah! My daughter! I am very glad to see you; come, come here, do your duty and submit your own wishes to your father's will. I have made up my mind to teach your mother how to behave herself, and, as an earnest of this, here is Martine, whom I have brought back, in spite of her, and reinstated in the household.

HENRIETTE. Your resolutions deserve praise. Take care, father, not to change your present humour; be firm in carrying out what you have resolved, and do not let anything lead your good nature astray; do not give way, do your utmost to prevent my mother from mastering you.

CHRYSALE. What? Do you take me for a simpleton?

HENRIETTE. Heaven forbid!

CHRYSALE. Am I a fool, pray?

HENRIETTE. I never said so.

CHRYSALE. Do you think me incapable of the strong convictions of a rational being?

HENRIETTE. No, father.

CHRYSALE. Have I not spirit enough at my time of life to be master in my own house?

HENRIETTE. Yes indeed.

CHRYSALE. Or am I so weak-minded as to let my wife lead me by the nose?

HENRIETTE. Why no, father.

CHRYSALE. Bah! What do you mean then? You appear to be making game of me to speak to me like this.

HENRIETTE. If I have offended you, it was unintentional.

CHRYSALE. My will should be implicitly obeyed in this house.

HENRIETTE. Indeed it ought, father.

CHRYSALE. No one has any right to give orders here but myself.

HENRIETTE. Yes, you are right.

CHRYSALE. It is I who hold the position of head of the family.

HENRIETTE. Certainly.

CHRYSALE. It is I who can dispose of my daughter.

HENRIETTE. Oh! Yes.

CHRYSALE. Heaven has given me supreme control over you.

HENRIETTE. Who has said anything to the contrary?

CHRYSALE. And I mean to show you that when you take a husband you have to obey your father in the matter and not your mother.

HENRIETTE. Ah! There you grant my most earnest desires. My only wish is that you will insist on obedience.

CHRYSALE. We shall soon see whether my wife will dare to oppose my wishes . . .

CLITANDRE. Here she is, bringing the notary with her.

CHRYSALE. Now all of you support me.

MARTINE. Leave it to me, I will take care to encourage you if you need it.

Scene iii

PHILAMINTE, BÉLISE, ARMANDE, TRISSOTIN,
THE NOTARY, CHRYSALE, CLITANDRE, HENRIETTE,
MARTINE

PHILAMINTE. Could you not alter your barbarous style and draw up a contract in beautiful language?

THE NOTARY. Our style is excellent. I should be a blockhead, Madam, if I tried to change a single word.

BÉLISE. Ah! What savagery in the very centre of France! But at least, out of deference to learning, Monsieur, be good enough to express the dowry for us in terms of minae and talents rather than in crowns, livres and francs, and, in dating the contract, use the words ides and kalends.

THE NOTARY. I? Madam, if I were to grant your requests I should be hooted at by all my fellow lawyers.

PHILAMINTE. We complain in vain against this barbarism. Come, Monsieur, sit down and write. Ah! Ah! That impudent wench dares to show her face again? Why, pray, have you brought her back to my house?

CHRYSALE. Presently, at our leisure, we will tell you why. We have another matter to attend to now.

THE NOTARY. Let us proceed with the contract. Where is the future bride?

PHILAMINTE. The youngest daughter is the one who is going to be married.

THE NOTARY. Good.

CHRYSALE. Yes – there she is, Monsieur; her name is Henriette.

THE NOTARY. Very good. And the future husband?

PHILAMINTE. That gentleman is the bridegroom.

CHRYSALE. And that gentleman is the husband I intend her to have.

THE NOTARY. Two husbands! That is one too many.

PHILAMINTE. Why do you stop? Write down the name of Trissotin as my son-in-law, Monsieur.

CHRYSALE. Write down the name of Clitandre as my son-in-law, Monsieur.

THE NOTARY. Agree among yourselves and come to a ripe judgement between you which gentleman you intend to be the future husband.

PHILAMINTE. You must follow my wishes in this matter, Monsieur.

CHRYSALE. You must do what I tell you, Monsieur.

THE NOTARY. Come, tell me which of you I am to obey?

PHILAMINTE. What? You oppose my wishes?

CHRYSALE. I will not permit my daughter to be run after simply for the sake of the wealth in the family.

PHILAMINTE. People think a lot of your wealth, I must say! A wise man does not demean himself to be anxious on that score.

CHRYSALE. Well, I have chosen Clitandre to be her husband.

PHILAMINTE. And I have chosen this gentleman to be her husband: my choice shall be followed, I have made up my mind.

CHRYSALE. Really! You carry things with a high hand.

MARTINE. It is not for the wife to dictate; I think women should always knock under to men in everything.

CHRYSALE. Well said.

MARTINE. If they gave me notice a hundred times, I should stick to it that the hen should not crow in presence of the cock.

CHRYSALE. Quite right.

MARTINE. And we know that everybody jeers at a fellow when his wife wears the breeches.

CHRYSALE. That is true.

MARTINE. If I had a husband, I tell you, I should like him to be master in his own house; I should not care a bit for him if he were a ninny; and if I nagged him, or thwarted him, or made too much row, I should expect him to take me down a peg by a jolly good hiding.

CHRYSALE. You speak very sensibly.

MARTINE. Master is quite right to wish a proper husband for his daughter.

CHRYSALE. Yes.

MARTINE. Why should Clitandre be rejected? He is young and good-looking. And why, if you please, tie her to a scholar who is always writing poetry? She wants a husband, not a pedagogue; and as she does not wish to know either Greek or Latin, she has no need of Monsieur Trissotin.

CHRYSALE. Very good.

PHILAMINTE. We must endure her chatter to its end.

MARTINE. Scholars are no good except to lay down the law from their armchairs; I repeat it a thousand times over, I would never have a learned man for my husband. Learning is of no use at all in housekeeping; books do not harmonise well with wedlock; and if ever I plight my troth I shall choose a husband who wants no other book than myself, who does not know A from B – no offence to Madam there, – and who, in a word, should only practise Greek to his wife.

PHILAMINTE. Has she done? I have listened patiently long enough to your worthy interpreter.

CHRYSALE. She has spoken the truth.

PHILAMINTE. Now, to cut all this dispute short, I insist peremptorily that my wishes shall be carried out. Henriette and Monsieur shall be united instantly; I have said it, I mean it: do not answer me; and if you have given your word to Clitandre, offer him the choice of marrying our eldest daughter.

CHRYSALE. There is a good way to settle matters: come, do you give your consent to it?

HENRIETTE. Oh! Father . . .

CLITANDRE. Oh, monsieur!

BÉLISE. One might indeed make proposals to him that might please him better, but we desire to set up a type of love which shall be as pure as the morning star: the spiritual side of one's being shall take part in it, but the carnal side shall be banished.

Scene iv

ARISTE, CHRYSALE, PHILAMINTE, BÉLISE, HENRIETTE, ARMANDE, TRISSOTIN, THE NOTARY, CLITANDRE, MARTINE.

ARISTE. I am sorry to disturb this joyful ceremony by the sad tidings I am obliged to bring you. It troubles me greatly to be the bearer of these two letters containing bad news for you: one, for you, comes from your solicitor; the other, for you, comes to me from Lyons.

PHILAMINTE. What misfortune can cause us such trouble as to justify anyone writing to us?

ARISTE. This letter, which you can read for yourself, contains news of one . . .

PHILAMINTE. *Madam, I have asked your brother to give you this letter, which will tell you what I dare not come to tell you myself. Your great carelessness in business affairs has been the means of causing the clerk of your advocate to neglect sending me necessary information, and you have finally lost the lawsuit which you ought to have won.*

CHRYSALE. Lost your lawsuit!

PHILAMINTE. You seem very much perturbed! I am not at all agitated by this blow. Pray show a less cowardly nature wherewith to brave the vicissitudes of fortune, as do I.

Your want of care will cost you forty thousand crowns; and you have been condemned to pay that sum, with costs, by order of the Court.

Condemned: Ah! What a shocking word, it is only fit for criminals.

ARISTE. It is wrong, of course; you are right to protest against it. They ought to have stated that, by order of the Court, they beseech you pay to immediately forty thousand crowns and costs.

PHILAMINTE. Now let us see the other.

CHRYSALE. (*reads*). *Monsieur, the friendship which attaches me to your brother causes me to take an interest in all that affects you. I am aware that you have placed your entire wealth in the hands of Argante and of Damon, and I have to acquaint you with the news that they have both gone bankrupt on the same day.*

Oh Heavens! To lose thus all my possessions at once.

PHILAMINTE. Ah! What a disgraceful outburst! Fie! All this is nothing. There is no such thing to the true philosopher as a serious reverse of fortune, no matter what he loses, there remains himself. Let us conclude our business, and cast aside your grief; his wealth will be enough for us as well as for himself.

TRISSOTIN. No, Madam: cease to press this matter. I can see that everybody is averse to this union, and I never like to coerce people.

PHILAMINTE. This reflection has come to you very suddenly! It follows very quickly, Monsieur, after our downfall.

TRISSOTIN. I am weary, at last, of so much opposition; I would much rather give up struggling further, I have no desire to possess an unwilling heart.

PHILAMINTE. I have hitherto refused to believe anything to your discredit, now my eyes are thoroughly opened.

TRISSOTIN. You can see what you like in me, I care little how you take my action. But I am not the sort of man to endure the shameful and insulting refusals which I have had to bear; I am worth much more appreciation than is shown me, and I decline with many thanks to be allied to one who does not want me.

PHILAMINTE. How plainly he has revealed his mercenary soul! How little like a philosopher is his conduct!

CLITANDRE. I make no boast of being a philosopher, Madam, but, believe me, I link myself to your fate, and I presume to offer you, with my person, what little fortune the gods have bestowed upon me.

PHILAMINTE. I am delighted, Monsieur, with this generous deed, and I desire to crown your love. Yes; I give Henriette to the greater affection . . .

HENRIETTE. No, mother: I have now changed my mind. Forgive me if I resist your wishes.

CLITANDRE. What? You refuse to make me happy? Just when every one is willing to consent to my suit . . .

HENRIETTE. I know how little you possess, Clitandre; I always looked forward to the time when, as your wife, I could both gratify my tenderest affections and improve your worldly position; but now that our condition is so different, I love you too well to burden you with our adversity.

CLITANDRE. With you, any fate would be happiness; without you, any fate would be insupportable.

HENRIETTE. Love, carried away by its own ecstasy, ever speaks thus. Let us avoid the pain of unseasonable regrets: nothing wears away more quickly the tie of affection which unites us than the worrying cares of life's necessities; it often happens that husband and wife take to accusing one another for all the wretched troubles which succeed to their bright days.

ARISTE. Is what we have just heard your sole motive for refusing to marry Clitandre?

HENRIETTE. Except for it my whole heart would leap with joy, I decline his hand only because of my great love for him.

ARISTE. Allow yourselves, in that case, to be bound in such beautiful chains. The news I brought you was false. It was a stratagem, a happy thought I conceived to further the course of your love, to take in my sister in order to make her acquainted with the character of her philosopher when he was put to the test.

CHRYSALE. Heaven be praised!

PHILAMINTE. My heart leaps for you at the chagrin this contemptible deserter will feel. His base avarice will be punished when he sees in what style this marriage shall take place.

CHRYSALE. I knew well enough that you would marry her.

ARMANDE. So then you sacrifice me to their love?

PHILAMINTE. It is not you who will be sacrificed to them. You have the support of philosophy, and can see with a contented eye the crowning of their devotion.

BÉLISE. He had better take care, for I am still in love with him; a sudden fit of despair often makes people marry one another to repent of it for the rest of their lives.

CHRYSALE. Come, Monsieur, follow out my instructions, and draw up the contract as I have told you.

End of Play.